Developing a Self-Evalua

Related titles:

What Makes a Good School Now?, Tim Brighouse & David Woods
Developmental Planning for School Improvement, David Hopkins
School Improvement, Martin Thrupp

DEVELOPING A SELF-EVALUATING SCHOOL

A Practical Guide

Paul Ainsworth

Online resources to accompany this book are available online at: www.continuumbooks.com/resources/9781855395367

Please visit the link and register with us to receive your password and to access these downloadable resources.

If you experience any problems accessing the resources, please contact Continuum at: info@continuumbooks.com

Continuum International Publishing Group
The Tower Building   80 Maiden Lane
11 York Road   Suite 704
London   New York
SE1 7NX   NY 10038

www.continuumbooks.com

© Paul Ainsworth 2010

All rights reserved. No part of this publication may be reproduced or transmitted in any form or by any means, electronic or mechanical, including photocopying, recording, or any information storage or retrieval system, without prior permission in writing from the publishers.

Paul Ainsworth has asserted his right under the Copyright, Designs and Patents Act, 1988, to be identified as Author of this work.

British Library Cataloguing-in-Publication Data

A catalogue record for this book is available from the British Library.

ISBN: 9781855395367 (paperback)

Library of Congress Cataloging-in-Publication Data
Ainsworth, Paul, 1973-
  Developing a self-evaluating school : a practical guide / Paul Ainsworth.
    p. cm.
  ISBN 978-1-85539-536-7 (pbk.)
  1. Educational evaluation. I. Title

  LB2822.75.A385 2010
  379.1'58—dc22

Typeset by Ben Cracknell Studios
Printed and bound in Great Britain by Bell & Bain Ltd, Glasgow

Contents

	Dedication	VI
	Foreword by Jonathan Sherwin	VII
	Foreword by Andy Coleman	VIII
PREFACE	How to Use This Book	IX
CHAPTER 1	Introduction	1
PART 1:	Self-Evaluation Tools and Techniques	11
CHAPTER 2	Lesson Observation	13
CHAPTER 3	Work Scrutiny	30
CHAPTER 4	Pupil Focus Groups	42
CHAPTER 5	Questionnaires	57
CHAPTER 6	Pupils Conducting Lesson Observations	70
CHAPTER 7	Analysing Statistical Data	84
PART 2:	Self-Evaluation in Practice	99
CHAPTER 8	Teaching and Learning Review Systems	101
CHAPTER 9	Self-Evaluation of Continuous Professional Development	119
CHAPTER 10	Using Self-Evaluation to Validate Progress	129
APPENDICES		149
	Useful Websites & Further Reading	163
	Index	165

Dedication

To my family, C, J and S for all your support

Thank you to J for the writing inspiration and to J and R for the wonderful examples of school leadership that I strive to emulate.

I would also like to thank all those teachers and educationalists with whom I have discussed education concepts in recent years. I would like to particularly thank Julie Upton for discussing 'Blink Reviews' with me, Joy Morgan for explaining her school's development of 'Teacher and Students Co-planning' and Sally Thorne for her thoughts on questionnaires.

I also wish to thank all my colleagues at Belvoir High School and those from our partnership, the Melton and Vale of Belvoir Secondary Schools, who have discussed ideas with me and shared their self-evaluation work.

I am grateful to Optimus Education (www.optimus-education.co.uk) who gave permission for me to adapt articles written by Trevor Brittan, published in the *Learning and Teaching Update* as Case Study 6.4 and by Matthew Savage and Dr Margaret Wood, printed in *Secondary Headship*, as Case Study 6.2.

Finally, I would like to thank the many colleagues at Continuum Press who have worked so hard turning my manuscript into the final book.

Foreword

Jonathan Sherwin
Principal Belvoir High School

It is easy to dismiss the concept of school self-valuation as being a centrally driven, bureaucratically led, tick box exercise that has nothing to do with the realities of working with young people and the societal baggage they bring with them into school. Indeed, in my younger days when I was working for Local Authorities, both in Advisory and as an Education Officer, I recall saying that I could evaluate the effectiveness of a school after being in the place for an hour and, in general terms, I believe I was probably right.

Nonetheless, I was unconsciously applying evaluation criteria. I was observing relationships, the quality of the environment, the sense of purpose in all areas of the school. Above all, I was listening to staff and pupils, taking their comments at face value and asking the question, 'How do you know?' This broad brushstroke approach actually proved very effective. What it did not provide, however, was any solutions about how to address improvement.

This is a criticism often laid at the door of the Ofsted inspection regime but, in reality, it is the staff *and pupils* within the school who are best placed to drill down into its workings and outcomes: to analyse its performance, define the next steps and monitor and evaluate progress.

In this book, Paul Ainsworth provides a practical toolkit for self-evaluation at all levels of the school. The focus is on improvement and on addressing what will really make a difference. The philosophy which provides the framework for the book is firmly rooted in the heart of schools' core business, teaching and learning. Perhaps most importantly, all of the processes detailed throughout its pages draw upon the experience of the writer who has applied them in practice and knows they produce results.

Foreword

Andy Coleman
Senior Research Officer NCSL

Effective and rigorous self-evaluation is fundamental to the successful twenty-first-century school. In 2004, the *New Relationships with Schools* moved self-evaluation centre stage, making it a non-negotiable aspect of schools' accountability framework and fundamental in measuring the effectiveness of their day to day work (Ofsted, 2004). However, for the truly effective school, self-evaluation is an opportunity rather than a requirement, a chance to reflect on its beliefs, values and aims, and to take a long, dispassionate look at how far it is going to achieving these. Self-evaluation is critical to understanding 'the black box' (MacBeath, 1998, 2005) of what goes on inside the school, to identifying its strengths to build upon and its weaknesses to address – to aligning all of the school's efforts in the pursuit of its key, strategic priorities. From such a perspective, self-evaluation is a fundamental and non-negotiable part of the school improvement cycle.

School leaders in general, and Headteachers in particular, are fundamental to making this happen. Encouraging self-reflection and ongoing critique is the cornerstone of continuous self-improvement, so critical in helping schools keep up with the never-ending challenges and changes they face (Coleman, 2007). For the Head then, effective self-evaluation doesn't just mean making sure the Self-Evaluation Form is completed. Rather it is about seeking to establish the expectation that self-evaluation is a responsibility of all in the school. Such critical reflection is therefore a key part of the teacher's role, fundamental to their professional identify and a means through which they are empowered to actively develop their teaching craft to the support children's learning (Ruddock and Hopkins, 1985). However such a climate does not happen by chance and if such a consistent and ongoing commitment to self-challenge is to flourish, leaders must give attention to promoting a high trust culture in which openness and honesty are valued and weaknesses are viewed as a basis for learning and improvement (Bryk and Schneider, 2002, Coleman, 2008). In such a context, self-evaluation becomes a basis for collective endeavour, focused upon continuous improvement and driven by a deep-seated commitment to helping every child fulfil their potential.

But where to start? And what are the hallmarks of 'good' self-evaluation? As already indicated, the most effective self-evaluation is integrated into the school improvement cycle, not a one-off event, but rather an ongoing mindset which encourages reflection and continuous challenge by all. It is evidence-based but fit for purpose – self-evaluation is a means to an end and should not become a task in itself. It is also inclusive and should take into account the views of others, most notably the children and parents the school serves.

This book represents a valuable resource to anyone interested in school self-evaluation. It offers clear and practical guidance for teachers and school leaders on how to make the most of this process, keeping it manageable while ensuring that the evidence gathered is sufficiently robust to support practical decisions on how the school's operations may be improved.

References

Bryk, A. and Schneider, B. (2002), *Trust in schools: A Core Resource for Improvement*. New York: Russell Sage Foundation.

Coleman, A. (2007), 'Leaders as Researchers: Supporting Practitioner Enquiry through the NCSL Research Associate Programme', *Educational Management Administration & Leadership* 35, 479–497.

Coleman, A. (2008), *Trust in Collaborative Working: The Importance of Trust for Leaders of Sschool Based Partnerships*. Nottingham: NCSL.

Macbeath, J. (1998), *Effective School Leadership*. London: Paul Chapman Publishing Ltd.

Macbeath, J. (2005), *Self Evaluation: Background, Principles and Key Learning*. Nottingham: NCSL.

OFSTED (2004), *A New Relationship with Schools: Improving Performance through School Self-evaluation*. Nottingham: Department for Education and Skills.

Ruddock, J. and Hopkins, D. (1985), *Research as a Basis for Teaching*. London: Heinemann Educational Books.

PREFACE

How to use this book

Developing a Self-Evaluating School has been written so it can be read in different ways, according to the experience and needs of the reader. You may choose to read it in a linear fashion from the beginning to end and, as a result, you will build up a full practical knowledge of how you can immediately begin to develop the processes of self-evaluation in your school or in your role. You may already have a specific issue which this book will help you address.

Following Chapter 1, the introduction, the book is divided into distinct halves. Part 1 takes you through the main tools of self-evaluation, with a practical school-based approach and Part 2 looks at how schools have used these tools in a holistic fashion. If you do not want to read the book from cover to cover, why not read Chapter 1? Then you can dip into chapters which immediately take your interest.

Each chapter has been divided into three sections: The Basics, The Detail and Review Your Learning. If you just want an outline of a certain tool or reason for self-evaluation, read The Basics. The set of questions at the end of this section entitled Identify Your Starting Point will help you relate the tools to your own school or role and to decide if you want to read The Detail at that time or move straight onto the next chapter. Within the section called The Detail you will find descriptions of how you can use a specific tool or a certain type of self-evaluation. You will also find case studies of how real schools have developed their own self-evaluation and Pause And Reflect, which are further questions to help you to expand your skills in that area. The Review Your Learning section of each chapter recaps what you need to know and includes a set of key questions, enabling you to consider the issues in the chapter.

You may have a more specific purpose in mind. Perhaps you need to develop a school evaluation system, you are reviewing the continual professional development in your school or you wish to evaluate your extended school. In which case, why not move straight to the relevant chapters in Part 2 to find how schools and individuals have successfully used the tools of self-evaluation in a coherent system for these purposes, among others? Once you have done this, return to Part 1 for the explanations of how you can implement the tools in more detail.

Senior leaders

A Senior Leader may be particularly interested in how different self-evaluation tools can be combined so that teaching and learning can be reviewed in their school. The suggested route for such a reader would be to read Chapter 1 before studying Chapter 8. The questions in Chapter 8 will then help the reader to plan which other chapters from Part 1 they need to read in detail and in which chapters they can just read The Basics.

A Senior Leader may also be working towards a particular external award or may be tasked with reviewing a certain element of the school's provision. This reader may begin with reading Chapter 1 and then focus on the case studies in Chapter 10 to discover which is the closest to the project they are working on. The ideas within these case studies should reveal to the reader which tools in Part 1 are the most appropriate for their needs.

A new Senior Leader who is seeking to develop a grounding in self-evaluation may find the most appropriate course is to read Chapter 1 and then focus on reading The Basics and the case studies in each of the chapters of Part 1.

Middle leaders

A Middle Leader is likely to be most interested in tools which can enable good self-evaluation of their team. The most obvious chapters to begin reading would be Chapter 2 on observation, Chapter 3 on work sampling and Chapter 7 on data. Once the Middle Leader has begun to use these tools in the self-evaluation of their section of the school, they may begin to use a wider array of self-evaluation from Part 1. A Middle

Leader may also wish to see how some Senior Leadership Teams are combining the self-evaluation tools to review school performance and hence study Chapter 8 in Part 2.

Practitioner researchers

There will be some readers who wish to research the effectiveness of their own practice, whether for an academic course or for their own interest. In which case, after reading Chapter 1, Chapter 5 on questionnaires and Chapter 4 on focus groups may be good places to start as these do not require the assistance of other teachers and can give the researcher an opportunity to gain a good range of data.

End note

Above all, I wrote this book to be a practical, user-friendly guide. I am a teacher first and foremost and have written a book that will be relevant for members of a Senior Leadership Team, Middle Leaders and teachers so they can conduct their own self-evaluations. I hope this book will not sit idly in a bookcase but, instead, will be on your desk, well thumbed and filled with scribbled notes.

CHAPTER 1

Introduction

Self-evaluation in your school: SEFs, SERs and SIPs
Schools have always conducted some form of self-evaluation. In the past the formality or methods may have differed greatly between schools, as indeed may have the purpose. Many teachers' perception of self-evaluation will have been formed by the annual lesson observation by a senior member of staff. 15 years ago, when I began teaching, I presumed that my first school did not do any self-evaluation as in my first five terms the only time I was observed was by the new Headteacher who wanted to get to know the staff. In hindsight, this was not the case but it is still an interesting perception to hold.

Today the term self-evaluation is difficult to avoid. Senior Leaders can feel the SEF (Self-Evaluation Form) is a constant millstone around their necks, especially if a visit from OFSTED is looming. It is not uncommon to hear of Headteachers of large schools working from home as they update their SEF. For Headteachers of smaller schools, some of whom have large teaching commitments, the demands of completing the SEF can be a considerable concern. In turn, Middle Leaders can become weary of a Headteacher's constant reference to the SEF, especially if they have been given the task of writing a department SEF (a document they may not see as their responsibility). Teachers who have not been given this task may simply wonder what all the fuss is about: after all, in a school year the average secondary teacher writes 200 pupil reports and surely an SEF is just the Head's version of this?

Regional contexts

In English state schools self-evaluation for OFSTED has been a formal part of the Headteacher's role since 1993 and of the Headteacher Statement. This was revised in 2001 as the Self-Evaluation Report and in 2005 became the Self-Evaluation Form.

In Wales, Estyn has the responsibility for inspecting the quality of standards of education and training in the principality. Headteachers have the option of completing the Self-Evaluation Report (SER) but it is not compulsory. Inspectors are instructed to ask for a copy of the SER and, if one is not available, it is suggested that the Inspector uses the most recent school improvement plan as a basis for the inspection. Schools that have not produced a SER will be asked how they monitor and evaluate achievement and progress.

Her Majesty's Inspectorate of Education (HMIE) is the Scottish equivalent to OFSTED. There is no requirement for a pre-inspection written report. Instead, at the start of the inspection the Headteacher is invited to use a one-hour meeting to brief the inspection team on the impact of their approach to improvement through self-evaluation, which also covers the outcomes for all learners who attend their establishment. In the independent sector, the Independent Schools Inspectorate (ISI) also provide an optional form, called the SEF, for schools to use. They comment that schools who do use this process have found it helpful. The ISI does, however, state that they do not require schools to follow particular patterns of self-evaluation.

Although not all sectors of education in Great Britain formally require a self-evaluation document to be produced, all school leaders will be asked in some form how they evaluate the progress at their school.

Self-evaluation for Senior Leaders, Middle Leaders and practitioners

The best school leaders will want to evaluate not only their progress over the years, but also the day to day standards in their school, as without this information it is not possible to improve. Clive Woodward said of his winning World Cup rugby team that he looked for a hundred things and then tried to do them all one per cent better. His first task was to identify those hundred things that he wanted to improve upon.

Today Senior Leadership Teams are bombarded by new initiatives and it is not possible, nor desirable, to implement them all. Instead, they must identify which are the most appropriate to increase the standards of attainment at their school. This can only be done accurately by having thorough knowledge of the current strengths and weaknesses at their school.

Schools must also identify their training needs to determine the programme of Continual Professional Development (CPD) planned for the academic year. It is easy for Senior Leaders to become so involved in a particular issue that training can be repeated year after year. One example of this in many schools can be Special Educational Needs training, where the same topic is tackled year after year at the same level and, as a result, staff can resent the training. Thorough self-evaluation would identify the gaps in staff knowledge and ensure the training moves people's practice forward.

The first experience a group of Senior Leaders may have of self-evaluation may be writing the audit for a specialist school's bid. The bid is unlikely to require evidence of how the self-evaluation has been conducted but schools must complete detailed analysis of the strengths and weaknesses of their specialist subjects. It can be tempting to write an audit which matches the plans the schools may wish to implement through specialist status. The obvious danger of this is that the school may introduce innovative proposals that do not actually address weaknesses at the school so the standards of attainment do not improve either in the specialist subjects or across the curriculum.

There has also been a growing expectation for those colleagues who hold Teaching and Learning responsibility (TLR) points to conduct self-evaluation, whether they have pastoral or curriculum responsibilities. This has occurred in parallel with their roles being renamed, changing from middle management to Middle Leadership. One of the expectations of leaders is that they establish a vision for the future. Middle Leaders need to evaluate the work of their team if they are to find the correct path forwards. The first self-evaluation many Middle Leaders may have conducted are the numeracy and literacy audits beloved by the national strategies, which began in 2000.

In addition, Middle Leaders have responsibility for the performance management of the staff that they lead. If meaningful targets are to be set for their colleagues they need to have a good idea of the strengths and weaknesses of those teachers. This requires a more systematic evaluation procedure than the yearly observation which has started to become tradition in many schools. Furthermore, some Headteachers now expect Middle Leaders to verify whether their staff are ready to pass through the Upper Pay Spine threshold or move up it. If this system is to prove resilient, Middle Leaders must have evidence on which to base their opinions and provide that evidence to back up their recommendations.

Self-evaluation is not just about structures, hierarchy and bureaucracy. Those teachers who really want to develop their craft in the classroom recognize they must have the ability to identify how effective their teaching methods have been in their pupils' learning. Some teachers may move this a stage further forward so that is becomes a research project, either for an academic course or for their own intellectual interest. In many ways the self-evaluation of one's practice as a teacher is at the heart of the process which Donald Schön described in his work on reflective practitioners (*The Reflective Practitioner*, Basic Books: 1983). For many educators this process is seen as cycle of events: description of events; the feelings and thoughts of the teacher; evaluating the experience; analysing the situation; considering what else could have been done and, finally, determining an action plan for future practice.

The dangers of self-evaluation

It is can be very difficult for teachers to be precise about what exactly happens in the classroom as our viewpoint is influenced by our emotions. Using the right self-evaluation tools will aid a teacher with this dilemma. The same issues can arise when leaders are trying to conduct self-evaluation but the effect can be much greater, due to the impact on a larger number of people. Without careful use of self-evaluation tools it can be very easy to reach incomplete, or even incorrect, conclusions by drawing only on the anecdotal evidence you have to hand or, alternatively, by considering data only. This is a classic scenario that can arise at Senior Leadership interviews when a candidate makes a statement about a school based their study of a data set and the Headteacher or governors become quite defensive as they have an explanation that contradicts the candidate's conclusions.

Many Senior Leaders will instinctively feel they know the strengths and areas for development of their school. However, it also true that, due to their role and place in the hierarchy, they may not see the day to day reality. In parallel, Middle Leaders will often complain that they know the strengths and weakness of their department and just need the time to put them right. Their diagnosis may be accurate but, as we have already seen, many outside agencies will wish to know how these conclusions have been reached.

Where to begin?

There is a huge wealth of evidence that can be drawn upon when we begin self-evaluation. In terms of statistical evidence we often feel we are drowning in a sea of acronyms – FFTs, CATs, YELLIS, APS and

CVA, to name but a few. In other areas we may feel we are relying just on opinion and do not have anything solid to base our views upon.

Figure 1.1: *Jargon buster*

FFT	Fischer Family Trust
CAT	Cognitive Ability Test
YELLIS	Year Eleven Information Service
APS	Average Point Score
CVA	Contextual Value Added

Thus the real art of self-evaluation is having a varied diet of methods which provides the evidence we need, whether it is for a governors' report or developing a submission for the NACE challenge award, but is also manageable within the confines of running a school, leading a department or teaching a subject. The best self-evaluation is often based on a triangulation of evidence, where a number of sources all point to similar conclusions. This is especially important if the self-evaluation is for internal evidence such as a senior team reviewing the performance of a department or a house. Middle Leaders will feel at best very uncomfortable or, worse, victimized, if they feel findings have been drawn from a single, potentially biased, evidence source. For Senior Leaders, who may be working on competency issues regarding members of staff, it is even more essential that there are no justifiable complaints of unfair practice.

A practical guide to self-evaluation

This practical guide is divided into two sections. Part 1 considers the different types of evidence that teachers and leaders can draw upon in self-evaluation. Part 2 shows how the tools can be used in different situations and school contexts. Further details of how the book is structured and the guidance it provides are outlined below.

Chapter 2 Lesson observation

Most teachers will think of lesson observations as a primary source of self-evaluation and, of course, in the previous rounds of OFSTED they were one of the major sources of data. Observations could be those produced as part of a Senior Leadership Team audit or by the Head of Department or Head of Year in their line-management role. They could also be part of a 'learning walk' where senior colleagues spend time walking around a school, watching portions of a number of lessons. The obvious difficulty of relying too heavily on this source of data is that they are just snapshots of a point in time. As all staff will recognize, the strengths or weakness observed may be one-offs contrived by a mixture of circumstances.

This chapter includes guidance on:

- The varied uses of lesson observation and how they can be incorporated into a coherent system
- How to conduct high quality lesson observation, record evidence and present feedback
- How inspections intended for self-evaluation can feed into coaching structures and CPD planning

Chapter 3 Work scrutiny

Work scrutiny is more commonly referred to in many schools as book checks. However, with the inclusion of work in folders or artefacts, the term 'work scrutiny' is more accurate. An interesting consideration regarding work scrutiny is whether the observer concentrates on studying the output of the pupils or the teacher, the marking. Many teachers perceive it is the latter and as soon as they hear of a book check they anxiously try to put as much red pen on the pupils' work as possible, in an attempt to show diligence beyond the call of duty. It can be fascinating for the scrutinizers to compare the work of one pupil in a range of subjects. However, it can be even more interesting for teachers to see how the output of a pupil can vary in different lessons.

The chapter includes guidance on:

- How to carry out work scrutiny effectively without being swamped with evidence
- The advantages of planning the recording template in advance
- How work sampling is affected by the growth in Virtual Learning Environments and IT systems to store pupils' work

Chapter 4 Pupil focus groups

The use of pupil focus groups is increasing rapidly in schools and they are now an integral part of the OFSTED process. Focus groups are semi-structured interviews of a group of pupils. Teachers may feel justifiably nervous about the opinions their classes will present of their teaching as they may feel that malcontent pupils will use it as an opportunity to settle scores. However, in all the pupil focus groups I have conducted this has never been the case. In fact, pupils tend to give very considered and intelligent feedback and one way of convincing teachers of this is to allow them to watch video footage of the focus group session.

This chapter includes guidance on:

- How to use focus groups effectively in schools
- How to set up a focus group, record the evidence and summarize the findings

Chapter 5 Questionnaires

Schools have conducted questionnaires on pupils' views for a considerable length of time. Some Local Authorities even conduct and analyse pupil questionnaires themselves and compare a particular school's results with results from across the county. Questionnaires also form part of the data gathered by value added testing, such as YELLIS. Some schools develop their own questionnaires to research a particular topic, such as the effectiveness of a pupil discipline system. They are also the form of self-evaluation that Middle Leaders are more comfortable using and are often used by classroom practitioners researching their own practice, either for an academic course or out of intellectual curiosity.

That chapter includes guidance on:

- How to write your own questionnaires and how to ensure the evidence is gathered is useful and valid
- Managing the questionnaire process, including examples of questionnaires and the conclusions that have been drawn

Chapter 6 Pupils conducting lesson observations

One area growing in popularity is the use of pupils in self-evaluation where they may be involved in observing lessons. During interviews for teaching staff it has become common for the candidate to teach a lesson and then ask the pupils for feedback on how they feel the lesson has been taught and what they have learnt. In addition, some teachers who are researching their own practice will ask their pupils how effective the lesson has been. These two ideas have become formalized in some schools and pupils are observing lessons.

This chapter includes guidance on:

- How to set up systems for the effective use of pupils in evaluation
- How to train pupils while giving consideration to the ethics required to undertake such a process

Chapter 7 Data

This chapter could form a book in itself and perhaps one of the key decisions in a school is to limit the amount of data used, so people are not confused. This chapter reviews two groups of data: the more primary evidence of SATs, GCSE or A-level results and the set that is derived through some form of value added analysis, such as Fischer Family Trust, CATs, YELLIS or CVA data.

The chapter includes guidance on:

- How tracking mechanisms can be used by schools to make sense of data on a more regular cycle than an annual analysis

The final three chapters that form Part 2 review how self-evaluation tools can be used in certain situations.

Chapter 8 Teaching and learning review systems

This chapter shows how a school leadership team evaluates the progress that certain areas of a school are making. Schools may use departmental or faculty review systems or they may evaluate via year groups. It also covers the increasing need for schools to evaluate the progress of their wider provision, such as their extended services.

The chapter includes guidance on:

- How self-evaluation tools in Part 1 can be linked together to evaluate the work of a school, a key stage or a subject area

Chapter 9 Self-evaluation of Continuous Professional Development

This chapter considers how the findings of self-evaluation can contribute to planning a CPD programme and also how involving staff in self-evaluation can be a very valuable form of CPD. After all, it is no good knowing the strengths and weaknesses of your school if you cannot use this information to make progress.

The chapter includes guidance on:

- How self-evaluation tools in Part 1 can be applied to evaluate your CPD provision

Chapter 10 Using self-evaluation to validate progress

The final chapter of this book gives an overview of how schools can use their self-evaluation data to validate their progress. This can include a school evaluating its progress towards national agendas, such as the extended school or specialist school. This chapter also considers the evaluation of a certain aspect of school life – a school's pupil management system – and it considers a NACE Challenge Award in detail.

End note

There is no doubt that self-evaluation is a process that is here to stay. This guide will give you a practical starting point to build your skills and those of your school. It is certainly true that, whatever the stage of our career or our place in a school hierarchy, if we really want to make improvements we must objectively analyse the effectiveness of our performance. So, if you are trying to find out whether group work is really working in your lessons or if the intervention group you have implemented is proving successful or if a whole school reward policy is motivating pupils, why not use the tools in this guide and conduct your own self-evaluation?

PART 1

SELF-EVALUATION TOOLS AND TECHNIQUES

CHAPTER 2

Lesson observation

The basics

If you surveyed the staff from your school in the style of television programme *Family Fortunes* and asked them to name a method of self-evaluation used by schools, lesson observations would probably be at the top of the list. This is hardly surprising when you consider how widely used they have been. Lesson observation is often the first method of self-evaluation you meet as a teacher. Many teachers have been scarred by the experience of their university tutor visiting them on their teaching practice to observe one-off lessons, as the evidence from these few observations was so important in whether they passed or failed a teaching practice.

When I began my career in schools, a visit from Her Majesty's Inspectors would fill the staffroom with the same level of dread. The same has been true for the inspection process in the last three decades in every education sector, which placed lesson observation at the heart of the methods.

Unfortunately many teachers are terrified of being observed by one of their Senior Leaders and observations by Middle Leaders are not considered much better. The result of this, as many Senior Leaders will recognize, is that the topic of lesson observation can be one of the most divisive in any staffroom.

However, at the heart of self-evaluation is the challenge of how to ensure that high quality teaching and learning occur in every lesson.

This could be from the perspective of a Senior Leadership Team wishing to achieve this across every classroom, a Middle Leader looking for consistency across their year group or subject area or a teacher wishing to ensure their practice is consistently high. Lesson observations, on the surface, would appear to be the tool which goes to right to the heart of this challenge.

In addition to providing a method of self-evaluation observation should, and can, provide a real opportunity for the teacher to develop their practice and in any system of observations this needs to be constantly kept in mind.

If a Senior Leadership Team feels their self-evaluation processes are an area of weakness there is a temptation to immediately respond by implementing a cycle of lesson observations of the staff by the Senior Management Team. However these observations are presented to the staff, many teachers feel under pressure and believe the aim of the observer is purely to discover weaknesses in their teaching. Many teachers consequently spend hours planning their best lesson of the year. The result? The observer sees a fantastic lesson, the observer goes away reassured and includes the data in the self-evaluation record but the teacher's practice does not necessarily improve and it is unlikely that this is a true reflection of everyday life in the classroom. You would also expect that even the most successful and experienced classroom practitioner is likely to feel nervous in the presence of an observer.

In addition the process of observation can be stressful for the observer. In the first lesson observation I conducted as a young Senior Leader, I was asked to observe a highly experienced colleague who was acknowledged by the school as a leading practitioner. I was acutely aware that my judgements had to be completely accurate and I felt under pressure to ensure that the experienced teacher benefited from the experience too.

Identifying your starting point

1. How are lesson observations currently used in your school?
2. How do they integrate with other self-evaluation structures?
3. What is your opinion of how effective they currently are?
4. What is the general response of staff to lesson observations? Is there a culture of fear or a desire for improvement?

The detail
Organizing successful lesson observations
There are number of points which need to be considered before you begin a series of lesson observations:

- The cycle of observation, including which teachers will be observed
- Which staff will be observing?
- How will the observation be recorded?
- What is the duration of the observation?
- How will the issue of observation foci be addressed?
- Moderation of observations
- How can the observation be used to develop the quality of teaching and learning?

Cycle of observations
From a whole school self-evaluation perspective, before any sequence of observation is conducted it is important to determine a rationale for which teachers will be observed and over what time period. Is every teacher in the school going to be observed once or more than once? Another approach would be for a sample of teachers to be observed. This may be as part of department review system (see Chapter 8) or you may select teachers by some other criteria. The sample could include observing all the teachers new to the school or, alternatively, teachers who have been highlighted by other self-evaluation methods as having weaknesses or, indeed, particular strengths. Whatever cycle you use it is important to ensure that it is manageable and that you will stick to it. There is nothing worse than explaining a cycle of observation to your school and then not following it. Staff may highlight it as a lack of competence by Leadership Team or they may claim it represents victimization of, or favouritism for, certain individuals or they may see it as an indication that the Leadership Team is not interested in them or their subject.

CASE STUDY 2.1: ANNUAL CYCLES OF LESSON OBSERVATIONS

In one school the Senior Leadership Team conducted an annual cycle of lesson observations for every member of the teaching staff. At the beginning of each academic year the entire staff to be observed was divided between members of the Leadership

Team. The first criterion for this was that the Headteacher wished to observe all teachers who were new to the school or staff who, in the previous year, had been identified as having competency issues. The remaining teachers were shared among the other members of Senior Leadership Team with the only criterion being that they did not observe the same teacher they had observed in the previous year. Each Senior Leader then allocated their observees a week when the observation would occur, gave them a selection of availability slots and the observees then chose which lesson they wished to be observed for.

Strengths

This system is completely transparent and all the teaching staff knew their part in the process. In addition, the size of the school and of the Senior Leadership Team meant that each Senior Leader conducted one observation a fortnight, which was manageable. As all staff were observed, it was agreed to be a fair system.

Weaknesses

The system was not dovetailed with other self-evaluation tools so there was no triangulation. This meant it did not identify teachers who were only delivering a one-off lesson to a high standard nor did it give any benefit to those staff who found that observations were detrimental to their teaching. In addition, there was no progression for the teachers who were being observed from the previous year. Teachers could not build on the previous observation as the new observer was likely to have their own particular interest and had not read the feedback from the previous year.

Depending on the current situation of your school or your department you may feel that annual observations are not frequent enough. Perhaps you are leading a school which is graded as Satisfactory or you are under pressure from the Local Authority to improve standards and therefore feel that more regular observations are required. The same could be true if your school has implemented a new approach to learning and there is a desire to monitor its implementation.

If you are considering more regular observation it is important to consider how to integrate with other systems. One solution could be integrating it with performance management. Many schools write into their performance management schedules that each teacher is observed twice. If this is the case, why not use one of your self-evaluation observations to serve a dual purpose and provide evidence for these targets too? All that is required is that the Senior Leader conducting the observation should be aware of the teacher's performance management targets prior to the observation.

PAUSE AND REFLECT

- What cycles of observations currently exist in your school or area?
- What are the purposes of your observations schedule?
- How do they integrate with other self-evaluations structures?
- Do you keep to your schedule of observations?

Which staff should conduct the observations?
It is usually quite clear who should conduct Middle Leader observations. However, in larger departments or in large schools it is important that the Head of Department or Head of Year does not overload themselves as observations are a time-consuming commitment. Instead, the Middle Leader needs to encourage other people with Middle Leadership responsibilities to assist in observation and, indeed, pay to assist. For example, a Head of a Key Stage in a medium-sized secondary school could easily line-manage 18 people and observing each of these individuals lead a pastoral session is a larger commitment that many Senior Leaders, with much lighter timetables, tackle. In such circumstances the pastoral leader could consider asking Middle Leaders with different academic roles within this group to assist in the observations.

It should be assumed from the outset that Senior Leadership observations will not necessarily be conducted by those who have teaching experience in that subject. Instead, all Senior Leaders must develop the skills to observe across the curriculum and to give helpful advice. After all, a good observer will focus first on the learning that is occurring and, just as the pupils are not specialists in that subject and are expected to learn, so should the observer be able to identify if learning is occurring.

Indeed, you could even consider whether the observers need to be teachers. There is a growing number of professionals in secondary school who are members of the Senior Leadership Team but who are not teachers. Providing such an individual with the skills to observe will have the dual benefit of greatly increasing the capacity of the Senior Leadership Team while giving the individual added knowledge that will make them even more effective in their role.

CASE STUDY 2.2: SCHOOL BUSINESS MANAGER ASSISTING WITH OBSERVATIONS

The fact that School Business Managers (SBMs) don't have a teaching background can make their feedback of real benefit to a school. For example, within an OFSTED inspection team there has previously been a lay inspector who is not a qualified teacher. An SBM's observations may identify different issues than the observations of a qualified teacher but that makes them no less pertinent. Furthermore, in many schools the governors will have a rolling programme of department observation with the aim of building the knowledge of the governor linked to certain curriculum areas. Governors are always told that they should not reach conclusions about the quality of teaching and learning and this should not be discussed in any reports produced. However, it is only human nature to make such value judgements. The SBM may spot similar issues to a governor and discussing this after the lesson may be useful in helping the teacher to verbalize the rationale and benefits of the lesson.

An SBM's classroom observations perform a number of useful functions for the school. First, the Senior Leadership Team's ability to self-evaluate teaching is increased. The viewpoint of the SBM as a non-teacher can provide feedback from a different perspective and this can support teachers when they are observed by those with different backgrounds. This is in addition to the valuable knowledge the SBM will receive which will enable them to perform their role of School Business Manager more effectively.

The findings from observation and self-evaluation can be very valuable for the SBM in working with the CPD co-ordinator in setting and getting best value from CPD budgets. The best organizations take great care over their use of training budgets. However, sometimes, if a school budget is tight the tendency is to cut the training budget first. By being part of the evaluation system, the School Business Manager will have a greater understanding of the importance of particular training issues for the school's improvement and hence the importance of budgeting for those issues when helping the Headteacher to set the school budget.

Secondly, it can very valuable for the SBM to see how resources are used to aid teaching and learning in the classroom. This can be vital knowledge when setting budgets. For instance, in one secondary school both the Headteacher and the School Business Manager perceived installing interactive whiteboards to be an expensive luxury. However, had the SBM seen the quality an interactive whiteboard could bring to lessons, they then may have begun to reconsider.

On a different scale is the consideration of department capitation. Departments receive varying levels of funding. In some cases the logic behind this is transparent but in other cases it is less obvious. During a lesson observation the School Business Manager will see these resources being used in practice and this will give them further understanding of why each department's capitation is different. In addition, the SBM may be able to give feedback on how the resources could be used most cost effectively. An obvious example could be in the debate between the merits of photocopying or purchasing a textbook. The Business Manager may conclude it is more cost effective to increase the level of funding for a department for a single year to purchase textbooks on the understanding that funding would be reduced in subsequent years as the level of photocopying needed would correspondingly be reduced.

In addition, the SBM may observe there are items purchased by a department that sit idle in the classroom and could discuss with the department why this is the case. It could have been due to a lack of planning as to how the resource could be best used. In future when the department's leader were to bid for additional items, the SBM would be more able to assess whether the department leader had thought through how the resource could be best utilized. In some circumstances the Business Manager may suggest this is done in more detail before the product is purchased. At this point the department leader may realize it is not an efficient purchase and decide they do not actually need it. Or they may integrate the resource more carefully in schemes of work so it will be well used once it is received.

> **PAUSE AND REFLECT**
>
> - Who conducts observations at your school?
> - Who is available to assist with observations?
> - What training would they require to conduct meaningful observations?

What judgements will arise from the observation?
One of the key aspects of lesson observation is what outcome the observer is expecting to gain. This leads to considering how this feedback is applied to the self-evaluation schedule that observation forms part of. In some ways the answer to the question of what outcome is expected from an observation is a debate of summative or formative assessment.

If you are concerned about a forthcoming inspection then you may feel pressured to concentrate the observation on determining an inspection grade for the lesson, perhaps using the four-point scale of Outstanding, Good, Satisfactory or Unsatisfactory. This is, of course, an example of summative assessment. If the observation is to be used in a coaching cycle or as evidence for a research project you are likely to be more interested in highlighting the areas of strengths within the lesson and the areas of development. Perhaps in a Middle Leadership observation, you may be looking for a combination of the two. The Middle Leader will gather evidence on the quality of learning in the department using the inspection but will also wish to give valuable feedback to the teacher, thereby raising their confidence and making them consider how the lesson could be made even more effective.

A third type of judgment that may arise will occur if you are looking at a particular focus in the lesson. If you are an experienced teacher working on a particular area of your teaching you may wish someone to observe you with that particular focus in mind. If the observer is solely concentrating on one issue it can be difficult to consider the wider strengths and weaknesses of the lesson or to give an inspection grade.

How will the observation be recorded?
Once you have determined the type of judgement which is being gathered the manner of recording the observation needs to be decided. It is, of course, possible to video record the lesson but, in addition, the observer, whether it be the teacher analysing their own performance or another observer, will wish to record something on paper. It is at

this point that the observer is beginning their analysis of the lesson and beginning to make judgements.

If the observer is concentrating on determining an inspection grade, there are documents which separate a lesson into four processes: teaching, achievements and standards, assessment, and attitudes and behaviour. For each of these processes there is an explanation of what will be happening for each of the four inspection grades of Outstanding, Good, Satisfactory and Inadequate. In Figure 2.1 the grade descriptors are shown for the achievements and standards element for a lesson. (See Appendix 2.1 for the entire document.)

Figure 2.1: OFSTED *grades for the achievements and standards in an observation lesson*

Outstanding	Students are engrossed in their work and make considerably better progress than may be expected. They consider difficult ideas and are willing to tackle challenging topics. Achievement is very high.
Good	Most students make good progress compared to their starting points, meeting challenging targets and achieving high standards. Most groups of learners, including those with learning difficulties and disabilities, make at least good progress and some may make very good progress. Learners are gaining knowledge, skills and understanding at a good rate.
Satisfactory	Most students' learning and achievement are at least satisfactory. Students understand what they are expected to do.
Inadequate	A significant proportion or certain groups make limited progress and underachieve. The pace of learning is insufficient for satisfactory gains in knowledge, skills and understanding. Overall, standards are not high enough.

Some observers will simply shade in the grade boxes which are most appropriate to the lesson and then consider which grade has occurred most often in order to determine the overall grade. To make this method slightly more formative the observer may also jot down some notes against the boxes so that the teacher can understand why these judgements have been made. This is a very mechanistic style of recording. It provides some formative feedback to the teacher, in that they can also see the information for varying inspection grades, but it is unlikely that the teacher will receive good feedback from this type of observation. It is highly suitable for a teacher going through competency proceedings when the school is looking for evidence to show that the teacher is not competent. It is also useful if you are trying to gather evidence on the overall quality of teaching and learning prior to an inspection or for a School Improvement Partner (SIP).

The other extreme of lesson observation recording is for the observer to transcribe what they see occurring in the lesson, what the teacher and the pupils are saying, doing and writing. This is the type of observation that many teachers are accustomed to. However, the observer is not necessarily doing any analysis at the same time, so this needs to be done afterwards.

This way of recording lesson observation can be tweaked slightly so that the observer has two columns on the transcription sheet. (See Appendix 2.2) One column is headed 'Factors Promoting Effective Learning' and the other is headed 'Have You Considered?'. The observer writes down the events in the lesson in either column. It is then relatively straightforward at the end of the lesson to look at these columns and then collate them into two groups of bullet points, focusing on the strengths and weaknesses of the lesson. See Figure 2.2 opposite for an example.

This method of recording is very useful for the teacher in identifying how they can improve their teaching. Valuable evidence can be gathered across a group of observations of strengths in teaching within a school and can also highlight areas the school needs to work on as a whole. However, some observers can find it difficult to relate this information to an inspection grade if one is required.

Duration of observation
There used to be an expectation that an observation would last the entire length of the lesson. There are many circumstances when this is a good use of time but, increasingly, observations now consider sections of the lesson. The National Strategies and the three-part lesson plan played a part in this change. When teachers began to use the three-part lesson plan, it was the starters and the plenary sections which required the most work. Therefore, rather than observing the entire lesson, Middle Leaders and consultants would observe one or both of these sections of the lessons but not be present for the middle section of the lesson. This was particularly useful if the Middle Leader wished to conduct some moderation with the consultant of what they had seen.

A similar process was used by Initial Teacher Training tutors who were anxious to check that the student's mentor was not being overly

Figure 2.2: *A completed lesson observation pro forma*

Copies to: Assistant Head, Line Manager, Curriculum Leader, Observee

Name of Observee: P Smith   **Date of Obs:** 8th January

Observer: P Ainsworth   **Class/Set:** Year 8AM
                                 Subject: Maths

Performance Management Target/Focus
Effective use of starters
(Above to be completed by observee)

The observer can consult the Middle Leaders Handbook *for criteria to be considered*

Time	Factors promoting effective learning	Have you considered?
	e.g. Planning, Pace, Challenge, Classroom Management, Differentiation, AFL Pupils queued outside classroom. Pupils came in quietly. A worksheet was on the desk. Pupils were told the starter was number races, they had to write start number and then do an operation such as add on 4. When they had written a certain number down they put their hands up. Pupils enjoyed the activity and it was making them think.	Could the pupils not quickly sketch the table in their books? Could you randomly check other books so that you know the accuracy of those pupils who don't finish first?

harsh or too lenient. It would often be a good use of time for the observers to leave the classroom for a discussion of what they had seen so far. This had the added advantage that the student teacher would then have the class on their own for an element of the lesson and there would not be the concern that pupils were behaving in a certain manner due to the presence of the Middle Leader.

Similarly, if the observation is for a performance-management target, rather than the observer watching for a whole lesson, the observer might instead arrange with the teacher the most appropriate moments within the lesson to attend in order to best help the teacher with their targets.

As the role of the School Improvement Partner has grown, one good use of their time has been to participate in learning walks with the Headteacher or other Senior Leader. Headteachers have been concerned that SIPs have purely concentrated on the data to draw their conclusions and set targets and, as a result, have been unaware of the good practice within a school or the problems with which the Senior Leadership Team have been dealing. During a learning walk the observer will walk through a number of classrooms, perhaps spending five or ten minutes in each classroom, generally looking for the presence of certain elements of the teaching. They may be looking at the on- or off-task behaviour of the pupils, whether pupils are discussing their work, how the teacher has structured the lesson, whether their aims and objectives are clearly presented. Some schools have made learning walks a formal part of their self-evaluation processes.

CASE STUDY 2.3: 'BLINK' WHOLE SCHOOL REVIEW

King Edward VI School has developed a blink whole school review. This is where lessons are observed for very short periods of time, often less than ten minutes.

The school had previously undertaken a whole school review which took the best part of a week. Staff were observed for full lessons and got detailed feedback but the school felt the process did not move the staff on as far as they wished and they required a review which looked at the School Development Plan themes and how they were impacting in the classroom. The teaching staff expressed a concern that observations taking place over a whole week created a tension that was not improving teaching and learning nor allowing them to address consistency.

The Leadership Team spent a long time looking at the themes that they felt could be reasonably judged in just five minutes. They also considered how opinions could be formed which were both snap judgements and yet maintained consistency in what Senior Leaders felt in those moments. Part of this was in giving lessons an OFSTED grade in this short time period. The Senior Leader honestly said this was achieved through gut instincts and, in some cases, it may be incorrect. There was an admission that the progress aspect was obviously the Achilles heel as this can never be assessed in a five-minute slot, whereas aspects of enjoyment, differentiation, focus and learning environment can be.

Initially the Leadership Team were all involved in the blink review system. This meant the team were all aware of the process and the standards that were required. However, increasingly, a 'crack team' of four, who are embedded in developing teaching and learning, have taken on the mantle of the blink reviews.

There was some concern from staff over how judgements could be based on the short time span but there was also an appreciation of how it could give the Senior Leadership a litmus test of the school in action and a realistic yardstick to consider globally how the school was improving the consistency of some key issues. Staff did feel that the blink review system was less pressurized than the previous formal review week which felt like an old version of OFSTED.

What are the strengths of the blink review system?

Time taken is small, yet results are helpful to assess what progress the school has made in its development. It allows the Senior Leaders the time to get to work on improving things rather than constantly measuring them.

What are the weaknesses?

There will always be an element of inconsistency between those reviewing. In addition, with the short period of observation, if something goes wrong this can make the staff member feel disappointed and disheartened that they have not shown their best.

See Appendix 2.3 for the pro forma.

The new style of OFSTED leans heavily on these shorter forms of observation. The Inspector is trying to moderate the judgements of the Headteacher, which are given in the SEF and there is not the time nor the manpower to observe all the teachers for full lessons so, instead, a learning walk is likely to be conducted. This may be done with the Headteacher so the Inspector can ask the Headteacher's opinion of the learning that they have seen taking place.

> **PAUSE AND REFLECT**
>
> - What different lengths of observation are used in your school and for what purpose?
> - Do you need a new pro forma for different lengths of observations?
> - How can you use different lengths of observations within your self-evaluation processes?

Observation foci

In discussions of observations the subject of observation focus is never far away. As we have seen there are occasions when having a solid focus can greatly aid the quality of observation, such as if it is intended to evaluate a performance management target. However, if the observation is intended for more general purposes the presence of a focus can disrupt the observer.

> **CASE STUDY 2.4: AN OBSERVATION FOCUSING ON KINAESTHETIC LEARNING**
>
> In one of the first Senior Leadership observations that I conducted I discussed with the experienced teacher the idea of using a focus. I was slightly intimidated by the observation that I had been tasked with and the idea of discussing a focus with the practitioner before the lesson was intended to begin to reduce any antagonism that may have been present.
>
> The focus that was decided on was to determine the level of on- and off-task behaviour by the pupils in a kinaesthetic-style lesson and also to see if there was any difference according to gender. I observed each pupil in the class for one minute and at ten-second intervals I made judgements as to what the pupil was doing. Were the pupils on-task or off-task listening, writing and

> discussing? I then repeated the process. These 12 judgements of each pupil were collated and analysed according to how long the lesson has been running and the gender of the pupil and were cross-referenced with the lesson plan. These findings were then discussed with the teacher who was very intrigued about how the pupils behaved at certain points in the lesson. The discussion did have good pedagogical value in promoting professional dialogue.
>
> However this method of observation was not really suited to the purpose of the observation which was a Senior Leadership round of lesson observations. I was so intent on applying the focus that I was unaware of other strengths and weakness within the lesson.

Focused observations do have real benefits especially if you are looking to develop a certain aspect of learning. However, it is difficult to conduct a general observation and provide a grade for a lesson at the same time as concentrating on a specific focus.

Moderation of observation
If you are introducing observations in your school using the OFSTED grading system it is very important to ensure that there is some moderation of grades. It is frustrating and, in some cases, deeply annoying for teachers if there is a real disparity in the grades that observers give to lessons.

Before gradings are used for lesson observations it good practice to have training on what these grades mean in practice delivered to all the staff. If you are teacher it is very difficult to deliver an Outstanding lesson if you do not know what one is. The next stage in developing a consistent grading system is for observers to observe lessons in pairs so that they can moderate each other's observation grading. This might be done over a full-length lesson observation, though this can intimidating for the teacher. A less intrusive method can be for a pair of observers to conduct a learning walk and spend 15 minutes in a classroom and then grade the lesson on what they have seen during that period.

To support this moderation process through the school it can become an annual event so that line managers conduct one joint observation with each of their colleagues during the year.

How can the observation be used to develop the quality of teaching and learning?
The obvious way to improve the teaching is by the observer providing thoughtful ideas for development. This places an onus on the observer

to keep up to date with the latest best practice. Unfortunately, Senior Leaders can often become so immersed in the pressures of running a school, that they may not have remained abreast of the latest best teaching practice as well as their classroom practitioners have done.

First, if excellent ideas, methods or lessons are observed, use a staff meeting to give these teachers the opportunity to present their ideas to colleagues. This could possibly called a teaching workshop. Secondly, produce a staff newsletter with articles written by teachers about lessons that have worked really well. Thirdly, if, in reading through a series of observations, you continually note the same problem or identify a common aspect absent from lessons, then arrange INSET on that subject. If it is an area that you are unfamiliar with, find a commercial course and either attend it yourself or arrange for a colleague to attend and afterwards provide a presentation for your staff on that topic. Lastly, if you are trying to develop a number of specific strategies in your school, explicitly communicate to the staff that the lesson observation will have these foci. This allows you to determine how effectively an initiative is being implemented and identify good practice, which you can then share.

Observations can be used in very different ways to improve teaching and learning if we move away from those conducted by senior management. Peer observation and coaching observation are two such opportunities.

Peer observation involves organizing opportunities for our colleagues to observe each other. In this situation the observer should be learning by seeing new methods and techniques in action. This can invigorate the staffroom in a much more cost-effective way than sending teachers on expensive courses. School management needs to be prepared to provide cover to allow this process to occur.

'Coaching' is a current buzzword that could be the subject of a separate book. Briefly, one method of using coaching in teaching is to identify strengths among your teachers, for instance using interactive whiteboards or classroom management. A teacher who wants to improve their interactive whiteboard use will then work with the coach whose specialism this is to plan a lesson. The coach observes the lesson and provides feedback. In this situation the teacher being observed will improve their practice. School management needs to cover the coach's lesson so they can work with the teacher in advance and observe the lesson.

These methods are very cost-effective and are rooted in sharing good practice. They could also have the knock-on effect of bringing the staff together and improving staff morale at the same time.

PAUSE AND REFLECT

- How does the data from lesson observations feed into sharing good practice and CPD planning?
- What benefits would peer observation bring to your school or area?
- How could you use coaching to improve teaching and learning?

Review your learning

There is no doubt that when used well, lesson observation is a very powerful tool. However, at the same time, it can be a very time-intensive process. It is also true that lesson observations can put teachers under considerable pressure so one needs to balance this viewpoint with the quality of data that you would acquire. It is important to ensure that, whatever system of lesson observation you implement, it is carefully explained to all staff so that no member of staff feels as though they are being targeted for any particular reason.

Lesson observation, when used carefully and sensitively, can also be a good vehicle of Continuous Professional Development not only for the colleague being observed but also for the observer.

For these reasons lesson observation is a tool that needs to lie at the heart of any self-evaluation process, yet at the same time, it must not be the only tool and there needs to be awareness that it is only a snapshot at a certain point in time.

Key questions

To decide if your use of lesson observations is effective, ask yourself the following questions:

1. What is your cycle of lesson observation?
2. How does this cycle link with other self-evaluation tools?
3. How are lesson observations recorded?
4. What judgements are made and how are these then used?
5. Can you use the evidence to clearly identify areas for CPD, not only for the individual, but for groups of teachers?

CHAPTER 3

Work scrutiny

The basics

The two methods of self-evaluation which are closest to the actual learning process are lesson observation and work scrutiny. If lesson observation considers how pupils are learning, then work scrutiny is a study of the product generated by the pupils.

Traditionally this was called a book check but, as we know, the progress generated by pupils is not shown only in exercise books. If the process is called a book check, some teachers will either get upset or complacent about the fact that, as their pupils do not write only in exercise books, not all commendable work by pupils is included. A better title would be 'pupil work scrutiny'. This could take into account work in folders, pictures, three-dimensional models, computer files and even audio or film records. Taking account of these less concrete representations does make scrutiny ever more complex. Initially subjects such as PE or Drama may not be included in this work scrutiny but will instead be looked at through lesson observation and pupil focus groups. In these subjects Senior Leaders are aware of the product through results on the sports pitches or performances on the stage.

A book check was often simply considered to be about looking at the teacher's marking. The frequency of marking would have been noted and a check made that the teacher had put red pen on each page so that parents would have no grounds for complaint. In reality, work scrutiny is more importantly about the quality of the pupils' and teachers' output and not the quantity.

Work scrutiny has become ever more important with the focus given to assessment for learning (AfL) in recent years. It is accepted that, appropriately used, AfL techniques are necessary to improve the quality of learning in schools and thus are an ingredient of Outstanding teaching and learning. The use of AfL can be evaluated via lesson observation and also by asking pupils during a focus group (see Chapter 4) if they know what they need to do to improve their learning. In addition, many would agree that identifying effective AfL can also be achieved by studying the written communication between teacher and pupil that is seen during work scrutiny.

In developing work scrutiny there are a number of areas which need to be developed:

- First, how is the work scrutiny to be organized? This will obviously vary according to whether it is conducted by a Senior Leadership Team, a Middle Leader or an individual teacher researching their own practice.
- Secondly, what is the focus of the work scrutiny? Without this careful planning the process, especially if it is from a whole school perspective, can rapidly become unwieldy.
- How will the work scrutiny be recorded? This needs to be linked to the focus and, again, if this is not tightly organized, work scrutiny can become an impossible task.
- It is also worth considering how the feedback will be presented to staff. Unlike a lesson observation, at Senior Leadership level it is likely that feedback will be given to a range of staff and may even be anonymous. The way the feedback is presented is likely to affect any improvements that may be made to the practice of the teachers.
- Finally, it is also worthwhile considering how you will look for improvement so that the work scrutiny becomes part of an ongoing process for improvement and not just a series of one-off actions.

Identifying your starting point

- What cycles of work scrutiny currently exist in your school or area?
- What are the purposes of your work scrutiny schedule?
- How do they integrate with other self-evaluation structures?
- Do you keep to your schedule of work scrutiny?

The detail

When you are planning and conducting work scrutiny the following four points need to be carefully considered:

- How it is organized?
- What is the focus of the work scrutiny?
- How will it be written up?
- How will feedback be presented to groups of teachers as well as to individual teachers?

Organization

There are many different ways of organizing a work scrutiny and from the beginning the key factor is how you plan for it. It is very easy to allow the process to escalate so it is unmanageable. There can be nothing more deflating than having a large pile of books and artefacts in front of you and knowing that, however you perform the scrutiny, it is likely to take you hours.

The initial task is to decide on the sample that you wish to take. This will depend on who is conducting the scrutiny and for what purpose. First, let us consider a Senior Leadership work scrutiny. The most detailed version of work scrutiny would be to sample pupils from each cohort of the school. One method would be to take six children from each year group, two of above average ability, two average and two below average, and to collect all their work from each subject. If your school is co-educational this should be from three boys and three girls. If we consider an 11–16 secondary school, this would be five year groups of six pupils all studying an average of ten subjects and suddenly we are looking at over 300 books, folders or artefacts. This would be a very lengthy process and, as such, is probably not effective.

At this point Leadership Teams may consider either using a longitudinal or latitudinal sample. A longitudinal sample might involve looking at one subject area and selecting a sample of pupils from each year group, possibly on the lines given above. In a primary school this could be an opportunity for the Headteacher to work with a subject co-ordinator and identify the progress that pupils are making through the school.

A latitudinal sample could look along the school, select a certain year group and review all the work produced by a group of pupils. In a large school this task could be conducted by a group of Senior Leaders, as it would consider the work from pupils taught by a number of teachers. In a primary school, the Headteacher may use this as an opportunity to work with one teacher by looking at the work produced by that one class.

Some people would argue six pupils is too many and that Special Needs pupils should also form a discrete cohort for their own work scrutiny, in which case a better sample for either a longitudinal or latitudinal study could be four pupils; one above average, two average and one below average. If this still seems too onerous for the size of your Senior Leadership Team you could even reduce the sample to three pupils.

Another method sample could be to look at a Key Stage. This may provide the opportunity to identify the progress that pupils are making as they move through the school and is more manageable than studying the whole school.

Any form of whole school work scrutiny can be a time-consuming task so consider who else outside your Senior Leadership Team could assist. This could be seen as a professional development opportunity for a colleague seeking Senior Leadership Team experience, a way of providing a whole school reference point for your literacy or numeracy co-ordinator or even a way of increasing the knowledge of teaching and learning of a non-teaching member of the SLT, such as the School Financial Manager.

Work scrutiny also provides an excellent opportunity for Middle Leaders to work with their teams. The longitudinal sample could be conducted by the subject leader with their team. This could be even become an annual event in which all your subject leaders use a meeting slot to conduct a work scrutiny and then feed back to the Senior Leadership Team.

PAUSE AND REFLECT

- How is work scrutiny organized in your school?
- Does it provide useful feedback?
- How could work scrutiny be organized to be more time efficient?

Focus

In many ways the focus should be linked to how the work scrutiny is organized and may actually govern the organization of the work scrutiny. The assumption of many classroom teachers, as explained in Chapter 1, is that a work scrutiny is purely a measure of their marking. The result is that the teachers try to quickly mark the books required for the sample in as detailed a fashion as possible. If the focus of the work scrutiny is the quality of the assessment provided by the teachers, then the SLT should be looking for consistency in using the school's assessment policy and the use of assessment for learning techniques.

However, it is likely now that a work scrutiny will be trying to identify the learning of the pupils. In doing this, it is likely that the quality of assessment will be considered. One question that could be asked is, are the pupils making progress during the year? For each subject the person conducting the scrutiny will be looking for evidence of progression. This is obviously a simpler task if the book has been marked diligently with grades of levels identified and suggestions for improvement clearly communicated – in other words, assessment for learning in practice. This can be difficult if teachers are less experienced in their use of AfL and this can in itself form useful feedback.

Many independent secondary schools and prep schools do not use National Curriculum levels. As a result, an issue that may be highlighted is the difficulty in measuring whether pupils are making progress over the year or if different subjects are challenging the pupils at very different levels. This could become an area of development for a school. How can the consistency of challenge be measured across the school?

Work scrutiny can also provide an opportunity to consider the effectiveness of the teaching. Two questions that can be looked at are:

- Is there a variety of activities so pupils can use different learning styles?
- Is there evidence of differentiation for pupils of different abilities?

One of the advantages of considering these questions via a work scrutiny, rather than lesson observations, is that this is not a snapshot of one lesson at a certain time. Instead, the evidence is gleaned over a longer period of time and cannot be affected by a teacher trying to do something different for a one-off lesson.

A continual issue for many Senior and Middle Leaders is the amount of homework set. In any year it is likely that leaders will be told by some parents that too much homework is being set and, inevitably, they will hear the opposite too. A work scrutiny could focus on homework and consistency within the school policy by considering questions such as:

- Is homework being regularly set?
- What appears to be the duration of the homework?
- What types of homework tasks are set?
- Does homework aid the learning process?

Of course if the work is not clearly labelled as homework then it is impossible to answer these questions. Therefore, if there is a perception that homework is an issue in your school or subject and you wish to use a work scrutiny to analyse this, it is important that for a period of time before the scrutiny teachers instruct their pupils to label their work. Maybe this could then become part of the homework policy.

Another set of common foci for work scrutiny can be those connected with the literacy strategy. Many schools have recognized that an important factor in raising the attainment for boys at the end of each Key Stage is improving the quality of their writing. Primary teachers have always seen that all curriculum activities provide an opportunity for writing. In secondary schools there can be a temptation for some teachers to consider that literacy is an issue solely for the English department. A work scrutiny provides a good opportunity to consider the consistency of both pupil performance and teacher response to many literacy issues. These could include continuous writing, presentation, handwriting, and balance between word/sentence level and text activities.

CASE STUDY 3.1: WORK SCRUTINY WITH A FOCUS ON CONTINUOUS WRITING

In an 11–16 school considerable energy and time had been given to developing continuous writing as this was seen as a weakness of the boys in the school. This was seen as even more important in raising whole school attainment due to the number of boys in the school. The school had already conducted book checks on a termly basis. This was developed to have a focus on literacy. Book checks had been conducted by the Senior Leadership Team which consisted of five colleagues. For this book check the Principal chose to include the newly appointed literacy co-ordinator. The sample size was six pupils from one year group which meant each scrutinizer could concentrate on one pupil. A pro forma was developed with a list of questions for each curriculum area and included:

- Are there opportunities for continuous writing?
- Does the pupils' writing show progression?
- What is the standard of presentation?
- Are there opportunities during homework for continuous writing?
- Is the assessment consistent with the literacy policy?

The group made a list of key points for each question.

The main finding was that there was little consistency across the curriculum. One of the difficulties the group found was in how to give more detailed feedback to Middle Leaders as there was one pro forma for each pupil rather than one for each subject. The work scrutiny would have been more effective if the information had been collated on a spreadsheet and then sorted so each Middle Leader could have been given a copy of the comments for their subject only.

Whatever focus is chosen for the work scrutiny, it is often fascinating to note how a pupil's presentation in one subject can be so different to that in another. Or how a so-called weak pupil may be making minimal responses in English yet write up a science experiment with clarity and flair.

Writing up
Of all factors related to a work scrutiny, probably the key to making it effective is to have carefully considered the manner in which it will be written up. Without carefully planning this section of the project you may find the work scrutiny can become very difficult. Schools often develop their own pro formas for recording their findings and may have different grids for different purposes. For instance, a Senior Leadership work scrutiny may be written up in a different style from that used by a head of department or subject co-ordinator. The best pro formas are developed over time and it is likely that the first one that you will plan will be changed over time.

When designing a pro forma we need to consider the focus for the work scrutiny that has been identified and to break that focus down into a series of key questions. The set of questions can be placed in a grid where comments are then written.

CASE STUDY 3.2: ASSESSING THE QUALITY OF HOMEWORK

A school makes the decision that the quality of homework needs to improve across the school. Curriculum areas have used meeting time to discuss effective homework that can be set. The Headteacher wishes to gather feedback from Middle Leaders of how effective this improvement has been. At a Middle Leaders' meeting a set of common questions is identified which can be considered by all curriculum areas (as listed in the focus section above). Each Middle Leader has to complete the grid (see Figure

3.1) for a sample of five pupils. The questions are open-ended so one of the Senior Leaders completes the table to show the Middle Leaders the type of responses that are required.

One of the conclusions reached was that all teachers had to ensure that the pupils work was correctly dated and labelled otherwise it was difficult to scrutinize.

Figure 3.1: *Pro forma looking at homework quality*

	Pupil A	Pupil B	Pupil C	Pupil D	Pupil E
Is homework being regularly set?	Homework every week.	Homework is not set every week but reasonably regularly.	Homework is set but little work is dated.	There is no evidence of homework.	Homework is set but not completed judging from teacher comments.
What appears to be the duration of the homework?	There would appear to be at least 25 minutes.	Variable length, some very short piece, a couple of sentences and also full-page pieces.	Generally short sections, e.g. five-sentence answers.	Cannot tell.	Cannot tell.
What type of homework is being set?	Mainly continuous writing.	Variety: comprehension, brain storms, diagrams and short essays.	Mainly comprehension or labelling diagrams.	Cannot tell.	Exercises from the textbook.
Does the homework develop the learning process?	Seems to develop themes shown in classwork.	Not always consistent with lessons but teacher comments indicate progress.	Looks to be mainly recap of the classwork.	Cannot tell.	Cannot tell.

If the work scrutiny is looking at the work from a sample in a year group it is likely that there will be more than one person conducting the process. You need to decide if you will have one sheet for each subject. In this case it is relatively simple to feedback to Middle Leaders. However, this method does not then show the difference in pupils' work across the curriculum which can often be fascinating and raises some interesting questions. Perhaps the solution that makes the most sense is for one person to look at each pupil but to compile the work scrutiny on a spreadsheet, so each pupil's results can be collated and each subject can be separated out to provide feedback to Middle Leaders. When there is more than one person conducting the work scrutiny, it is also worth considering coding the feedback or asking fewer open questions so that it is easier to draw together the results.

> **PAUSE AND REFLECT**
>
> - Have you developed a consistent style of pro forma for work scrutiny?
> - How time consuming is it to complete?
> - Does the pro forma encourage consistency from the scrutinizers?
> - Is it straightforward to draw conclusions from?

Feedback

When you are conducting your scrutiny it is important to consider how you will feedback your findings. If you are conducting a whole school work scrutiny, there are likely to be two choices. The feedback on the findings could be of a general nature to the whole staff or it could be separated out for different subject areas. It is unlikely that individual feedback is given to colleagues. If the work scrutiny is conducted by a Middle Leader, overall conclusions could be given to their team or it could be individualized.

Whichever format is decided upon, it is probably worth considering a few simple guidelines. As with lesson observations, start with the positive features you have found within the work scrutiny. It is not good practice to feedback on every issue you have noticed so, instead, consider the most significant issues. These could be areas that you are already working to develop or just the priorities that you have identified. Within the issues that you have identified consider what advice could be given on how these could be improved.

Often one of the most helpful pieces of feedback that can be given on work scrutiny is that it is not about teachers working harder and longer, rather it is about teachers using the same amount of time but working smarter, so that their efforts are more effective. Even though it is likely that in your work scrutiny you will be looking at a host of teaching and learning issues, many teachers will think it is about their marking. One of the best outcomes of a work scrutiny can be in the sharing of good practice, particularly if you can identify methods which are effective and make marking speedier. Nearly all teachers, whatever their level in the organization, are interested in such tips.

If the work scrutiny is concentrating on assessment there is another type of feedback that can be given, and that is to use OFSTED grades. This can be particularly useful if you are working with a colleague undergoing competency proceedings or working to pass their Qualified Teacher Status and you consider in either situation that assessment is an area of weakness. Grids or pro formas have been designed which provide illustrations of practice which are linked to the four OFSTED judgements. Figure 3.2 has been designed by www.effectivemarking.co.uk and it would be relatively straightforward to look at the statements and decide which were the most appropriate for a colleague's marking. They would receive very clear feedback on their assessment and could look at the grades for suggestions on how they could improve their practice.

Whichever kind of feedback you are providing, the aim should to promote improvement in teachers' practice. It is important to provide support, if required, for individual colleagues or subject areas where a weakness is identified. It would also be unreasonable to expect huge changes to be made so, therefore, small steps in progress should be looked for. Teachers need to know that this is part of an ongoing cycle and to be made aware of the date or timescale for the next scrutiny. Finally, at the time of the next scrutiny, do not start from the beginning. Instead, study the previous findings and look for development. It can be useful to highlight previous findings to colleagues at a set period of time before the next scrutiny, in case they have been forgotten amid all the other happenings in a busy school.

PAUSE AND REFLECT

- Who are you feeding back to?
- What format will the feedback take?
- Are both positives and negatives identified?
- Is support provided where improvement is required?

Figure 3.2: *Using OFSTED grades in work scrutiny. (Reproduced with permission of Effective Marking™)*

Outstanding
Strategies exist to acknowledge/celebrate the achievements of targets

- Children are involved in setting targets for improvement
- This is a very good level of response to personalized comments from the teachers
- There is some subsequent response from the teacher
- Comments from the teacher are particularly focused and diagnostic, revealing very good subject knowledge
- Children actively demonstrate understanding of targets set

Good
All children are set relevant, accurate targets on a regular basis

- Self-assessment is a regular activity: children know what they are good at and know what they need to do to improve
- Children revisit and respond to previous learning through written, post-task questions
- Children respond to personalized comments from teachers

Satisfactory

- There is sufficient work in the children's books to allow marking to have an impact (reflecting a well planned curriculum)
- Work is marked regularly
- Children know how well they have done in relation to the objective
- Marking helps to build confidence
- The majority of marking is about recognizing success
- Some relevant targets are set
- The teacher's handwriting is easy to read
- The teacher's spelling and use of standard English are accurate

Inadequate
Marking is likely to be inadequate if it does little to help children to improve. The key features of inadequate marking are the opposite of satisfactory marking:

- Work is not marked regularly
- Children do not know how well they have done in relation to the objective
- Marking does not help to build confidence
- The majority of marking is not about recognizing success
- No relevant targets are set, targets are poorly chosen
- The teacher's handwriting is not easy to read

Review your learning

The art of triangulation is to look for findings highlighted across the survey. There may be a concern that pupils are receiving too didactic a delivery in one subject area. In a single lesson observation the teacher may do something different but, by considering the results of a pupil focus group and the work in books, it may become clear that the original concern was well founded. There could be unease that pupils are not challenged enough by a teacher. They may receive very favourable comments in a pupil focus group. However, if the lesson observation and the work scrutiny indicate otherwise, this could highlight a training issue for this colleague.

An effective work scrutiny will provide many different types of information. There should always be positive achievements to celebrate and is important that these are communicated. Specific classes, groups or individuals will be highlighted to need further attention or support. It is likely that areas for improvement will also be identified and these could include planning, resources, expectations, teaching, marking, assessment, attitudes, engagement and motivation and, finally, performance and progress through school. Lastly, the work scrutiny should provide you with a set of layered targets (smaller stepping stones) as well as longer term curricular or whole school targets.

With any type of self-evaluation, the Senior Leadership Team should not be using the gathered evidence as a stick to beat people with but should be considering how the school needs to develop, either through whole school INSET and development planning or by changing individual colleagues' practice so it becomes more effective. The challenge for any Senior Leadership is to ensure that everybody in their school reaches their full potential – pupils and teachers alike.

Key questions

To decide if your work scrutiny is effective, ask yourself the following questions:

1. Do you have a sample that is manageable?
2. Do you know what you are looking for?
3. Does the sample cover a range of pupils?
4. Is there a clear pro forma to complete?
5. Can you analyse and link various aspects of the information?
6. Can you use the evidence to clearly identify areas for development?

CHAPTER 4

Pupil focus groups

The basics
Focus groups are widely used in the world of advertising and in politics to try to gain insight into the views of consumers or voters. One early experience of focus groups being used by schools is in the independent sector where school leaders have worked with marketing agencies to utilize focus groups to learn the opinions of parents so the schools can develop plans to increase pupil numbers. During recent years of OFSTED inspections it has been normal for Inspectors to gauge the opinion of the student body through a discussion with a group of students. The sessions have, in effect, been focus groups but were not initially referred to by this name.

Focus groups are further away from the actual learning process than either lesson observations or work scrutiny and, instead, are based on the opinion of the pupils who attend lessons. Therefore focus groups do have to be used with great care and, if your school is using focus groups for the first time, it is likely that a number of staff will feel uncomfortable about the process. We are often not used to pupils being asked for their opinions on their learning.

A focus group consists of a group of pupils who are asked a series of questions and their answers are recorded. Focus groups can either be organized so that each pupil is asked the same question in turn until they have all answered and then a new question is asked, or they can be more discussion-based – a question is asked and the pupils discuss their points. In some focus groups the questioner will stick strictly to the questions and in other scenarios the questioner will probe the pupils' responses to gather a greater understanding of their views. This is one strength of focus groups in comparison to written questionnaires.

In developing focus groups there are a number of areas which need to be considered. Some of these are very similar to those we considered when planning work scrutiny. First, what is the aim of the focus group and how will this affect the organization of the focus group? It is important to carefully consider which member of staff is conducting the focus group, be it a consultant, a pastoral leader or a classroom teacher, as this can impact upon the value of the focus group. The set of questions needs to be carefully structured with reference to the focus so the answers serve the purpose initially intended. The children need to be carefully briefed about the purpose of the group and its ground rules. How will the focus group be recorded so it is as effective as possible, with consideration given as how to the feedback will be presented to staff?

Lastly, with any form of self-evaluation it is important not to see the focus group in isolation, but also to know how the results will feed into an overall process. Focus groups should not be used as the sole source of information-gathering, but are best used alongside other evaluation techniques such as lesson observations, examination results, questionnaires, book checks and parental feedback to provide triangulation. Focus group data can also be compared with informal conversations held with pupils, staff and parents.

Identifying your starting point
Where are focus groups currently used in your school?

- How do they integrate with other self-evaluation structures?
- If they are not used, what are the barriers to their use?
- Where would appear to the most suitable place to use them?

The detail
Organizing a successful focus group
Key to running a successful focus group is the planning. The following factors need to be considered:

- The precise aim of the group
- The people involved
- How pupils are expected to behave during the focus group
- The questions asked
- The method of recording

- How the data will be analysed
- How the information will be shared

What is the aim of the focus group?
In some ways focus groups are perhaps one of the easiest self-evaluation tools for individual teachers to establish. As well as being used at a whole school level by OFSTED, they are just as likely to be used by an individual teacher conducting a personal research project. It is important to be precise about what you are aiming to evaluate during the pupil focus group. Try not to make this too broad. So, for example, for a gifted and talented (G&T) co-ordinator using a pupil focus group it may be very tempting to aim to evaluate the whole G&T provision. However, it may be both more appropriate and productive to instead consider an element of the school's G&T provision and concentrate on this during the focus group. The aim of the focus group in this scenario could be to study the appropriateness of the enrichment activities which are offered within the G&T programme.

CASE STUDY 4.1: STUDYING G&T PUPILS' VIEWS ON EXTRA-CURRICULAR PROVISION

A G&T co-ordinator in a secondary school was evaluating the quality of the G&T provision to provide evidence for a Challenge Award application. There was considerable evidence from whole school evaluation of the impact of the G&T provision within the classroom but there was a little evidence of pupils' opinions on the extra-curricular provision. The G&T co-ordinator chose to have a large group – ten pupils, two pupils each from Years 7–11 – to gain evidence from a larger cross-section of pupils. As this was a G&T focus group, the pupils were all on the G&T register. The G&T register had a larger proportion of girls to boys, approximately two to one, and this was reflected in the pupils chosen.

The focus group was conducted at lunchtime and to encourage the pupils to participate the school provided a buffet lunch. To provide a learning opportunity for additional G&T pupils, the G&T co-ordinator invited two Sixth Form pupils to take notes. As a back-up the G&T co-ordinator also made an audiotape recording of the session. The G&T co-ordinator also considered whether, if G&T focus groups were to become a regular evaluation activity, they could be led by Sixth Form pupils.

Questions

The pupils in the focus group were asked the following questions:

- What extra-curricular activities have you participated in this year?
- Which did you enjoy the most?
- Which helped your learning?
- Have any of the activities been specifically for G&T pupils?
- How did they compare with the other activities?
- What other activities do you think the school should offer?

The two Sixth Form pupils wrote up their summary of the focus group and this was presented to the Senior Leadership Team and Middle Leaders. Some of the evidence was also used to write an article considering the pupil benefits of extra-curricular provision at the school and pupils' ideas for the future, for the school newsletter.

PAUSE AND REFLECT

- How would you like to use focus groups in your school?
- Is this a for whole school, Middle Leadership or personal research reasons?
- What are you specifically trying to evaluate?

Who will be in the focus group?
There are two aspects to this question. First, which pupils will you select to form the focus group? Second, and just as important, who will conduct the interview?

At one school the Principal was very eager to take the interviewer's role for a Year 10 focus group to assess the quality of teaching and learning. However it was believed that the pupils might be reluctant to voice their opinions in front of the Principal. Instead the Head of the Sixth Form, who rarely had individual contact with pupils in this year group, ran the group.

At another school, where the quality of teaching and learning in an English faculty was being studied, an external KS3 literacy consultant, who was working in the school as part of the National Literacy Strategy, was used. It was hoped that pupils would respond honestly and openly to an impartial interviewer. (In fact they were touchingly loyal about their teachers!) They gave very useful information on possible improvements to teaching.

Similarly, if you plan to assess the quality of the G&T enrichment provision, the G&T co-ordinator may not be the best person to evaluate this with pupils as the pupils may associate the co-ordinator with the programme. Interestingly, in Case Study 4.1 the G&T co-ordinator did not see this as a problem as there was an extra-curricular co-ordinator in the school. Certainly though, the G&T co-ordinator would be appropriate if he or she were considering in-class provision.

CASE STUDY 4.2: THE REGISTRAR RUNNING FOCUS GROUPS

In one secondary school focus groups were implemented in the whole school evaluation system, yet there was a concern that the Senior Leadership Team did not have the capacity for this to become a regular occurrence. In addition, two of the Assistant Heads taught in the first department to be monitored, so they would not be appropriate choices to run the focus group. As a result, it was suggested that the school Registrar conduct the focus group. The Registrar said, 'It was good to be asked to conduct the group. It's often difficult to see things from a pupil/teacher perspective when you are dealing principally with the admin side. I think that, as a member of the non-teaching staff, I was able to take an objective viewpoint and be seen as a neutral observer by the pupils.'

The first pupil focus group was set up to include six pupils from Year 7. There were three boys and three girls, two able children, two middle ability children and two children who found academic learning difficult. The aim, though, was to select six pupils who would willingly articulate their opinions. The Registrar was given a list of questions which prompted discussion about the teaching and learning in the department. She chose not to tape or video the focus group but to make her own notes. She regularly interacts with pupils during the school day, continually helping them with their queries, but this was the first time she had worked with pupils on an issue related to teaching and learning. When asked how the pupils responded to her, she said, 'The pupils were initially a bit guarded because they weren't sure what was being asked of them but they soon relaxed and were willing to talk freely to someone who wasn't a teacher. They spoke frankly about lessons and staff but were never unkind or abusive.'

The success of the focus group was evaluated. When the process was analysed the Registrar said, 'The cross-section of pupils was good in some ways but occasionally meant that the more talkative ones (not always the bright ones!) wanted to take over the conversation and I had to make sure that everyone was able to have a say. However, I still think this is the best way. To have all pupils from one ability group would give a biased result and would not, therefore, be as valuable. Perhaps a group of eight would be worth trying to give a broader cross-section.'

The analysis of the data was particularly interesting especially as it covered the work of two of the school's Assistant Heads who, in previous OFSTED reports, had been identified as excellent teachers. In some ways it was a real strength that the Registrar conducted this focus group and that the results were seen as completely impartial. The major findings were that the pupils, on the whole, were happy at school and enjoyed their lessons. However the Registrar said, 'They were unsure of the significance of targets and levels. They didn't have a clear idea of what the levels were, why they were there, what they had to do to get to the next level or why. This seemed to apply across all abilities.'

The Registrar continued to take the role of leading pupil focus groups within the department maintenance check system. When asked how it had affected her work as Registrar, she explained, 'Seeing things from the pupils' point of view, getting a better insight into curriculum issues and into some of the difficulties teachers face has broadened my understanding of whole school issues which we discuss at Senior Leadership Team meetings.'

Numbers of pupils
In terms of pupil numbers, some people suggest using 8–13 people. However, many school leaders who have experience of running pupil focus groups find this is too large a group to manage and to gain each pupil's opinions successfully. You also need to ensure there are enough members of the group to create a dynamic as it can be very difficult to run a focus group if the pupils are not willing to speak. For this reason focus groups of fewer than four pupils can be ineffective. However, if you are a teacher investigating your own practice and know the pupils well and have a good relationship with them, you may gain good

information from four pupils. In general, many school leaders find that the most effective focus groups will be made up of 5–8 pupils.

If you are conducting a focus group with pupils from a single year group, six pupils can be a good number to work with. From this you can look to form a stratified sample, such as by keeping the gender ratio within the group reflective of either the school or the year group. As has already been indicated in the Case Study 4.1, there might be situation where the gender profile of the focus group is different from that of the school. If six pupils are chosen, you may decide to select two high ability pupils, two middle ability pupils and two less able pupils to give you a spread of viewpoints. It is important, though, not to use just pupil volunteers. You are looking for pupils who will articulate a range of opinions, not just the keenest, most enthusiastic, ones. This aspect of selection is a major difference from selecting for a work scrutiny evaluation. In the case of the G&T focus group you could present this as a speaking and listening masterclass so you may choose pupils who find the skills of self-expression difficult.

You may also find that pupil focus groups are less effective if you have a wide spread of ages. You may find that some of the younger pupils are too intimidated to speak with much older pupils present. You could also find that the older students are dismissive of the views of those younger than themselves.

Lastly, choose the time and location carefully. If the focus group is run after school or at lunchtime, will attendance be seen as a punishment? On the other hand, if it is run in lesson time, it is likely that teachers will complain that the pupils are missing crucial lessons. In some independent schools parents may also complain that their children are missing lessons that they have paid for. One solution is to hold the group in the meeting or training room so the pupils recognize it is an adult activity and feel that their views are important and will be respected. Pupils are often impressed if a nice lunch is provided but think about what young people prefer – a selection of pizza is likely to be enjoyed more than a buffet ordered from the local delicatessen.

Pupil behaviour
The first time pupils are involved in a focus group they will be unsure of what you expect. If you are conducting a focus group as a method of whole school self-evaluation it is important to set the ground rules in advance.

One consideration is whether the views of the pupils will be anonymous. If a written record is being taken of the focus group, this is likely to be the case. However, if you are using an audio or video record of the group and are considering playing elements of it to staff, you will have to explain this to the children.

Some interviewers take the concept of anonymity further by explaining that they will not accept any personal information about teachers. However, if the data is to be triangulated against lesson observations or work scrutiny, honest information from pupils can be extremely useful at a whole school level. In such circumstances it is important to explain to pupils what happens if they express a negative view about particular teachers. Perhaps the best way of tackling this with pupils is by explaining that focus groups are one method that is used to improve the school and the pupils' progress. It is often found that pupils are very reluctant to say anything negative about teachers. If they do, that could suggest there is a real problem that should be investigated.

PAUSE AND REFLECT

- Who will lead the focus group?
- What impact will this person have on the answers the pupils give?
- How many pupils will be involved?
- How will you choose the pupils?
- Will the pupils' views be anonymous?

Planning the questions

The next planning point is to be clear about the questions you will ask. How do your questions gather data which will be useful for the area you are investigating? The questions that you ask when you are evaluating the effectiveness of a behaviour-management system will be very different from those used to evaluate teaching and learning across the school.

While you are planning your questions it is important to consider how the questions will be asked. Will the interviewer read the questions out loud and then direct them at each pupil in turn? Will the interviewer ask a question and see who is first to answer and then allow the pupils to discuss their thoughts? Will the interviewer probe the pupils' responses? This is probably easier to do if the interviewer is involved in the school. However an outside consultant may wish to clarify points, particularly regarding jargon or expressions that the pupils use which are unique to their school.

CASE STUDY 4.3: CONSIDERING THE TYPE OF TEACHING

The Director of Studies of an independent school was trying to implement teaching and learning evaluation systems within the school. He was concerned that the diet of lessons the pupils received could often be dull, with little interaction, and would be likely to discourage pupils from staying on at the school to attend the Sixth Form.

The school had experience of running focus groups with parents in a bid to increase pupil enrolment so the concept of focus groups was not threatening to the senior management team, in the way that lesson observations were. The senior management team agreed to run a pupil focus group with Year 9 pupils with the aim of gathering their views on the quality of learning they were receiving. The Principal was eager to run the sessions but it was pointed out that his presence may inhibit the pupils so, instead, the Head of Sixth Form ran the session. Six pupils were chosen, three girl and three boys, two with high ability, two with low ability and two weaker pupils. The pupils were told that their views would be anonymous. The group took place in the Sixth Form centre which made it quite special for the pupils. It was run during an assembly and PSE slot, so that parents would not complain about their children being withdrawn from academic lessons.

The following questions were asked:

- What is your strongest/weakest subject?
- How do you know this?
- Which subject do you enjoy most/least?
- Why?
- What was the best/worst lesson you've attended in the last fortnight? Why?
- What learning activities do you enjoy most?

The Head of Sixth Form wrote a paper which briefly explained the main findings of the pupil focus group for each question and which included a few key questions from the pupils.

It is important to consider how much time that you have to run the pupil focus group as this will impact upon the number of the questions that you have time to ask. You will also need to consider how you will ask the questions. Will you ask each pupil the same question and work your way around the group so each pupil has the opportunity to answer the questions? Or will you ask the question and allow the pupils to discuss their answers? Sometimes during a focus group you begin with using the first method and, as the group dynamics form, you unconsciously move to the second scenario. Then your role becomes acting as a chairperson who is there to ensure that everybody in the group gets a chance to speak. You also need to decide if you are going to ask supplementary questions. These are often of major benefit to focus groups as they give you the chance to probe views further and clarify any potential misunderstandings. However, if a video recording of the group is going to be shown to staff you need to be sensitive about how your additional questions might be viewed by the audience.

PAUSE AND REFLECT

- What is the key aim of the pupil focus group?
- Do all your questions link to that aim?
- Have you got enough time to ask all your questions?
- How will you ask the questions?

Recording comments

It is important to consider how you will record the evidence of the focus group. You also need to consider what impact your chosen method will have on the pupils.

The most obvious method of recording is to simply make notes of the answers that the pupils give. If you have already prepared a grid which links to the questions then it is a simple process to complete it. This will also have the advantage of having the pupils' comments organized so that some level of analysis has already been completed. An example of part of such a table is included as Figure 4.1.

Figure 4.1: A focus group pro forma

	What is your strongest subject?	What is your weakest subject?
Pupil 1		
Pupil 2		
Pupil 3		
Pupil 4		
Pupil 5		
Pupil 6		

One difficulty in recording the results this way is that it can be challenging to listen to the pupil answers at the same time as trying to write them down. If the focus group is part of a whole school evaluation system, you could ask a member of support staff to record the answers. You may find that the member of staff enjoys the opportunity to be involved in a teaching and learning task. If it is a Middle Leadership task, you could ask your fellow Middle Leader or a second in department to help you on a quid pro quo basis. Or you could even ask a group of pupils to help you as the G&T co-ordinator chose to do in Case Study 4.1.

Some teachers have had good results with videotaping or audio taping and then analysing focus groups. This means that only one member of staff needs to be involved in the focus group, but students can be self-conscious at first when they are being recorded. There can be a temptation to transcribe the focus group as you will then have a full record of the group. However, it is important to bear in mind that transcription is a very time-consuming task and may not always be necessary.

Perhaps the most efficient method is to ask a colleague to make notes and at the same time make an audio recording of the focus group. This can be used as a back-up to clarify any points or misunderstanding later.

CASE STUDY 4.4: EVALUATING A DEPARTMENT'S PRACTICE

A secondary school was looking to introduce pupil focus groups as part of a faculty review system (see Chapter 8 for more details). There was a concern among the Senior Leadership team that staff would be suspicious of pupil focus groups. In parallel, the English faculty had been working with a English consultant from the Local Authority on developing speaking and listening throughout the school.

It was decided to ask the English consultant to run the pupil focus group so there could be no accusation of bias from staff. The focus group consisted of six pupils, one from each English class and, therefore, one from each teacher. A spread of different-ability children, three boys and three girls, was included. The focus group took place during an English lesson and the pupils were told that this was a good opportunity for them to develop their speaking and listening skills.

A video of the focus group was made as the intention was that extracts of the focus group would be shown in a future staff meeting. This would have a number of purposes: first, to show the staff an example of a focus group; secondly, to give an example of speaking and listening activity and, finally, to illustrate the pupils' opinion of assessment for learning.

The questions included:

- Can you describe an English lesson which you have enjoyed?
- What activities help you learn best?
- How much homework do you receive?
- What is your favourite/least favourite kind of homework?
- How often is your homework/classwork marked?
- What type of comments are the most/least helpful in improving your work?
- Do you know what grade your work would be if it were marked at KS3 SAT/GCSE level?
- Do you know what your preferred learning style is? Why do you think this?
- Do you think you should be taught just in your preferred learning style or in a variety of different styles? Why do you think this?

When the video of the focus group was shown to staff, they were surprised by the pupils' perceptiveness, admitting they placed more value on pupils' responses than they had anticipated.

The English department actually changed its marking policy, based on pupils' focus group comments. A decision was made to mark pupils' work less frequently but to set every pupil two clear targets for improvement each time exercise books were collected. Staff agreed that they felt that marking was less onerous, more focused and gave pupils much more practical advice on how to improve.

Analysing comments
The effectiveness of the focus group can only be measured by how useful the analysis is. It is important to note again that it can be dangerous to rely solely on evidence from a focus group and, before any action is considered, some triangulation should be conducted.

The interviewer could draw their own conclusions in a written document if the recording of the focus group is not easily understood by a third party. If there are open-ended questions it can be a good idea to code the pupils' comments. Coding is where the responses are grouped into similar categories. It can also be effective to try to distil the pupils' responses to some of the more objective questions into easy-to-digest statistics.

If the focus group is being used as part of a whole school evaluation system, the management group could read the transcript and draw conclusions. Or they could consider the information that is recorded in the grid. Obviously a more thorough method would be to see how the data relates to other data, for example lesson observations and exam data, already held. This is an example of triangulation which will be discussed in more detail later (see Chapter 8).

If the focus group is part of a Middle Leadership process, the Head of subject or year may look at the grid with their team and look to see how this impacts upon the teaching or pastoral support that they are delivering. In such a situation triangulation may not be required.

CASE STUDY 4.5: STUDYING CHILD SAFETY DURING THE SCHOOL DAY

A pupil focus group in a secondary school was conducted to determine where pupils felt most threatened during the school day. It was found that this was the pupil toilets and that pupils felt their unease increase during the day as the toilets became less cared for and dirtier. Following this research, the Business Manager considered the financial feasibility of employing a cleaner to work during school hours and keep the toilets clean. The school leadership team also hoped this would prevent the toilets being used for drug abuse. While these are not directly linked to children's learning in the classroom, there is undisputed evidence that, if these environmental concerns are addressed, pupils' behaviour is often improved and thus their learning improves too.

Sharing information

Lastly, it is important to consider how the results of the focus group will be shared with staff. As in Case Study 4.4, if the focus group has been videoed, this could be then edited and played at a staff meeting. This needs to be done very sensitively if pupils name specific teachers. However, this can be a way of explaining to staff the benefits of focus groups.

If the focus group is part of a whole school evaluation system on a particular subject area, a number of key points from the focus group may be communicated to the subject area. This could be in a similar fashion to key points shared following a lesson observation of three strengths and three areas for development.

If more detail is required a written report could be produced and presented. This can be useful if the focus group is taking a cross-curricular view, such as in Case Study 4.3. Some schools have their own in-house professional development newsletter. The G&T co-ordinator in Case Study 4.1 wrote an article for their school's newsletter which detailed the findings and provided information, with the hope that this could act as a catalyst for subject leaders to take action.

> ### PAUSE AND REFLECT
>
> - How would you record the results of your pupil focus group?
> - How will you analyse the results?
> - How will you share your findings with other colleagues in the school?

Review your learning

Establishing focus groups as a method of school self-evaluation has, undoubtedly, many positive outcomes.

While we think we know what is best for our pupils (and most of the time we do), it is fascinating to see if the energy and time we have put in to the activities we take for granted (marking, pupil self-assessment, target setting, setting homework tasks, and so on) are actually helping our pupils to make progress.

Perhaps the most rewarding result of focus group work is recognizing the confidence that pupils gain from articulating their opinions and feeling their views are being heeded. In Case Study 4.4 the Head of English explained that, 'One boy was clearly proud at having his views heard and talked for several terms afterwards about how much he had enjoyed "that interview I was invited to."'

While it is easy for schools to pay lip service to promoting a student voice (if you'll excuse the pun), pupil focus groups legitimately and purposefully involve pupils in a dialogue about their experiences as learners. This can only assist us in making those experiences more worthwhile.

Key questions

To decide if your use of pupil focus groups is effective ask yourself the following questions:

1 Do you know what you are looking for?

2 Do you have a sample which will give a variety of views?

3 Have you decided how you will record the information?

4 Can you analyse and link various aspects of the information?

5 Can you use the evidence to clearly identify areas for development?

CHAPTER 5

Questionnaires

The basics
Of all the methods of self-evaluation, questionnaires are the most widely used, both in educational settings and outside of them. Some schools have conducted questionnaires for a long time and, as a result, have a history of answers for the same questionnaire from over the years. Many organizations outside schools market questionnaires that schools can buy. They will set the questions, analyse the answers and present the schools with a set of findings. Such bodies include Centre for Evaluation and Monitoring (CEM), who produce YELLIS and ALLIS among others, and NFER, who produce a range of questionnaires. Some Local Authorities provide a similar service but without the cost. The only issue for the schools in such circumstances is that the Local Authority will have copies of the analysis and will use this to compare schools across the Authority.

Using a questionnaire is the least personal of the methods of self-evaluation in that the person who is conducting the self-evaluation is further removed from the subject of the research than in the three methods previously discussed. For this reason, they are also widely used by people conducting research, ranging from academics to student teachers. They can be a little like oil tankers – once they are underway they are very difficult to turn around. This gives rise to the danger that, if a questionnaire is badly prepared, the person using it only finds out once all the data has been gathered.

Even thought questionnaires are widely used in schools, they are rarely used by Senior Leaders to evaluate the quality of teaching and learning although they are often used to quantify pupil or parent opinions about wider school issues. However, teachers conducting their own research will often use questionnaires, even when it is the effectiveness of their practice which is being studied.

Identifying your starting point

- Where are questionnaires currently used in your school?
- How do they integrate with other self-evaluation structures?
- Are they used to study certain types of issues?
- How could they be used more widely in the school?

The detail

Organizing effective questionnaires

In common with the three tools of self-evaluation already considered, questionnaires are only fully effective following careful planning. The following factors need to be considered:

- The precise aim of the questionnaire
- The questions asked
- The number of pupils involved
- How the questionnaire will be completed
- How the data will be analysed
- How the results will be presented

The aim of the questionnaire

Researchers often find that poorly designed questionnaires can greatly hinder evaluation. It is important that the school leaders identify the key questions or areas for which evidence is required and ensure the questionnaire addresses these.

Before you begin writing a questionnaire, the first thing you should ask yourself is whether there is an appropriate commercially produced format available and, if there is, if its cost be justified. At the same time look at the questionnaires currently being completed in school, perhaps for the Local Authority or for another outside body, and see if the data that you require has already been gathered and, even better, if it has already been analysed.

If you have completed that process and the evidence is not already in school, you need to really tie down the precise aims of the questionnaire. It is often a good idea to develop a small number of key questions which address your key aims. Questionnaires can give so much data that is often unwise to create aims that are too broad. On the other hand, bear in mind that, if the survey is to be a census of the whole school population, it will not be popular among school staff if a second questionnaire is required to gather information omitted from the first.

CASE STUDY 5.1: DEPARTMENTAL CAPITATION

A School Business Manager was trying to ascertain whether the formula they had constructed to calculate departmental capitation was appropriate. When the school conducted a departmental review a tutor group in one year was asked to complete the following questionnaire on the subject:

- Do you regularly use textbooks?
- What condition are they in?
- Do you share textbooks or do you have your own?
- Can you take the book(s) home with you?
- Are photocopied work sheets regularly used?
- Are they re-used from other groups?
- How do these resources make you feel about your learning?
- How often do you use IT facilities?
- Do you use the internet or resources on the school intranet?
- Would it be useful to be able to access these from home?
- What other resources are used? DVDs? Specialist equipment? Data logging?

This would allow the SBM to consider how effectively the department's purchases in the previous year have been. Are resources regularly used or just hidden in cupboards? If bulk photocopying is being done could it be suggested to the Head of Department that it may be more cost-effective to consider the purchase of a textbook? Is the lack of ICT use due to a lack of resources or is the department not using those that they have? These types of findings will inform the School Business Manager's discussions with Middle Leaders about their level of capitation and will enable the School Business Manager to make more valued judgements about the bids put forward to them.

Formulating the questions

When you begin to formulate questions for your questionnaire, the starting point should be the key questions that address your aim. It is important to ensure that all questions in the questionnaire are linked to at least one of the key questions. It can often be easy to include questions that would give some interesting answers but are not linked to the key questions. This can result in questionnaires that are too long and onerous and, as a result, the pupils do not fill them in properly.

One factor that will have an impact upon both the questions that are asked and on the way that they are answered is whether the questionnaire is completed anonymously. It is often good practice for pupil questionnaires not to be anonymous. The comparison can be made with issues of disclosure relevant to child protection, in that children are always told that any information they give cannot remain anonymous.

The first point that needs to be considered when writing the questions is that they should not be leading or biased in anyway. It is surprising how easy it is to do this or to make assumptions about what students and pupils already know. The questionnaire needs to be carefully written in language appropriate to the young person who is completing it. If you are a secondary school teacher working on transition it may be worth asking the primary class teacher to check the questionnaire is age appropriate. It can also be difficult to design a questionnaire which is appropriate for students all the way from Year 7 to Year 13.

Within any questionnaire it is good practice to provide questions that give opportunities for different styles of responses. There is always a place for simple 'yes' or 'no' questions to quickly gather data. Often, though, the questions that are used most frequently are structured questions which give more detail but are still easy to analyse.

The 'Likert' scale has been developed for structured questions. Basically, this grades the responses into five groups: very negative, negative, undecided, positive and very positive. It can be a good idea to leave out the 'undecided' answer as there can be a tendency for many people to just select this option.

It can be very tempting to only use structured questions as these are far easier to analyse than open-ended questions. It is a good idea, though, to include open questions. They can act as a 'safety valve' so that, if people become frustrated with closed questions, they have an opportunity to write what they think. Open questions can also reveal information that you had not considered when the questionnaire was being designed. Open-ended questions can also be a good source of quotations to be included when the information is being shared.

It can be difficult to analyse the outcomes of open-ended questions as it is rare to find people giving exactly the same answers. In fact, if the same answers are given by two people, it is worth considering if one has copied the whole questionnaire from the other. The easiest way of conducting statistical analysis on open questions is to code them. This is achieved by placing the responses to questions in groups. One of the simplest coding methods would be to group open-ended question responses into positive, negative or neutral views.

It is important to always test the questionnaire on a small sample of pupils or teachers in advance to ensure both the questions and nature of responses is clear. Repeating a questionnaire because the first time around the questions were not clear is difficult to do. To test parent questionnaires I often ask support staff to help me by saying, 'Can you put your parent hat on for a moment?' Not only do they always provide valuable feedback, it often raises their self-esteem to be asked to contribute in such a way to school improvement.

PAUSE AND REFLECT

- What are the key questions which the questionnaire is researching?
- Is the language appropriate to the age of the respondents?
- Is there a variety of styles of questions, allowing for different responses?
- Are all the questions linked to key questions?
- Has the questionnaire been tested and did the respondents complete it satisfactorily?

Which pupils will be involved?

There can be a temptation to assume that all the young people in the school need to answer the questionnaire but this is not always the case. If the whole school completes the questionnaire you may find that many of the questionnaires are not completed properly and those forms cannot be included. It can be more effective to use a smaller group of young people but to have more control over how the questionnaire is completed.

Samples of young people can be effective but in these situations it must be ensured the sample is a stratified sample and reflects the make-up of the school or the group that you are researching. One simple stratified sample would be in a co-educational school that contains equal numbers of boys and girls. If you were being more precise, ensure that the sample includes equal numbers of children from each year group.

In a primary school it may be easier to use a few pupils from each class. The difficulty, though, is in ensuring that the questionnaire is fully understood by the youngest children as well as the oldest children. In a secondary school, it may be more straightforward to use one mixed ability tutor group from each year group. If the questionnaire is focusing on a particular year group, just one mixed ability tutor group may be chosen. If the results appear consistent that may be all that is required. If a particular system is being reviewed, a certain age group of pupils may be chosen if it is felt they may give the most useful response (see Case Study 9.1).

Completing the questionnaire
In schools questionnaires have generally been completed in three ways. If purely numerical data, such as the data required by a travel plan on how pupils have travelled to school, has been needed, often tutors have read the questions to their class and asked them to put up their hands. This is a good way of ensuring the questionnaire is completed, that pupils are clear on which answers to give and that special needs pupils do not need readers or scribes. Obviously this is unsuitable for more sensitive data.

The second method has been for the questionnaires to be given to form tutors or class teachers with the request that their groups complete them. This means that large amounts of data can be gathered quickly but the researcher cannot guarantee how it has been collected. Some teachers will ensure that the children complete the survey in silence while, in other classrooms, it can be a free for all which can affect the validity of the results. This is another reason why it might be easier to use a sample, rather than all pupils completing the survey.

The most time-consuming, but also most reliable, method is for a researcher to work with individual pupils, as a market researcher does. This method might be the only way of gaining meaningful evidence from very young children or those who are non-readers.

Increasingly, questionnaires can be completed on computers, which means they can be set up more quickly and analysis can be immediate. Schools that have implemented Virtual Learning Environments generally have a questionnaire feature on the VLE. When a pupil logs onto the VLE this can direct them straight to the questionnaire. The questionnaire can be set up so that all pupils are asked to complete it or the questionnaire can be directed at certain groups of pupils. The

VLE can keep a record of how pupils have completed their answers. A more simplistic version can be achieved via email, where a question can be sent to certain or all email addresses and the receiver has to click on a multi-choice answer.

In addition, there is specialist questionnaire software which means that, rather than putting the questionnaire on the VLE, it can be emailed to certain respondents and their answers returned straight back to you. Such advances mean that questionnaires are likely to be used more in the future than they are at present.

> ### PAUSE AND REFLECT
>
> - Which group of pupils do you intend to complete questionnaire?
> - When will they complete the questionnaire?
> - What impact will this have on the validity of the answers?
> - Is it possible to use IT to deliver the questionnaire to the pupils?

Analysing the data
It is important that while the questionnaire is being written careful consideration is given to how it will be analysed. For numerical or quantitative data there are many methods of displaying the data. The most popular are the different types of frequency diagrams or pie charts. These are often chosen so that, when findings are being fed back to groups of staff, they can be quickly and easily be understood.

Numerical results can also be used for analysis of factors such as the percentage of pupils who give certain answers. This method can be useful if comparisons are being made between different ages or genders of pupils.

Measures of central tendency can also be used. These are more commonly known as the average. It is worth remembering that there are three types of averages. There is the mode, or the most common answer. The median is found by arranging the data in size order and identifying the middle piece. The mean, which is the average most people think of, is calculated by adding up all the pieces of data and then dividing by how many pieces of data there are.

If open questions have been included in the questionnaire, it is these answers which can be the most difficult to analyse. If there is not an extremely large number of respondents, it may be possible to read all the answers and see if they begin to fall into natural groups which can then form the codes. The alternative is to derive a 'Likert' scale at the beginning of the process and then place the answers into these groups. One of the real benefits of open questions is that quotations which are given in answers to them can be used to highlight other statistics.

CASE STUDY 5.1: A TEACHER RESEARCHING THEIR OWN ASSESSMENT

Aim of the questionnaire

A teacher wished to look at the quality of assessment and the impact it had upon the pupils. This was motivated by two forces. The first was the teacher's Principal who often said that pupils just wanted to know two things from a teacher's assessment. These are the grade they are working at and advice on how they could reach the next grade. The Principal believed that praise has only a superficial effect on pupils. The second force was the lack of attention that most pupils paid to the marking of their work.

The teacher shared his objectives with the pupils by explaining he was researching their views about marking and assessment of their work. The pupils were asked to prepare carefully by considering what they had learnt and also to consider more deeply what impact these assessment comments had on their own learning.

A Key Stage 4 coursework assignment in which all the pupils had attained level 7 or 8 was selected and then the pupils' exercise books were randomly divided into three piles. Each group would receive a National Curriculum level and a comment. One group would have a tick and a one or two-word comment: either good, very good or excellent. The second group would receive a positive sentence about the piece of work, complimenting them on their high standards, their improvement or even their presentation. The last group would have a formative comment explaining what the pupils needed to do to reach the next level.

The teacher explained to the pupils that he was researching the effectiveness of his marking. Without discussing with their neighbour they were to read the comment and complete the questionnaire.

Questionnaire

1. Read the comment. Then circle two of the following words which describe how you feel.

Proud   Confused   Confident   Pleased

Unsure   Disappointed   Happy   Worried

2. What are your feelings about the lesson?

Very negative   Negative   Positive   Very positive

3. What type of comments would you like to receive?

_____

Analysing the data

There was little difference in how the pupils felt about the lesson. The pupils responded broadly positively to all three styles of assessment. However, when Question 1, which considered how the comment made them react, was analysed there was a noticeable difference, even though all the pupils had achieved a level 7 or 8. For the single comment of 'good', 'very good' or 'excellent', 100 per cent of the pupils circled positive words. For the encouraging sentence, 80 per cent of the words circled were positive. Yet, for the formative comment, less than 60 per cent of the words circled were positive. This appeared to be at odds with the Principal's viewpoint of assessment for learning.

When the pupils' free responses were analysed they were grouped into three sections. Almost 50 per cent of the pupils wanted to receive only praise or encouragement. Almost 40 per cent of the pupils wished to receive formative comments on how they could improve, but they all wished this to include praise too. In contrast, only 15 per cent of the pupils were prepared to accept formative comments that did not include praise.

The teacher felt that the major benefit of this piece of research was not the actual findings but the attentive manner in which the pupils engaged with the assessment. The teacher found that pupils often gave assessments a cursory glance in their eagerness to begin the next task or project. During that lesson and subsequently, however, pupils readily discussed their reactions to the marking of that piece of work and other assessments they had received. On that day, teacher and pupils alike reflected on their learning.

Presenting the results

With any type of self-evaluation it is important to consider how the results will be presented. If teachers are not going to be involved in distributing the questionnaire it can be useful to share the questionnaire with the teaching staff at the beginning of the process so there are no surprises or even conflict. Some staff can feel that questionnaires are secretive and are done behind their back even when that is patently not the researcher's intention.

When the questionnaire has been completed, the data needs to be presented in a range of ways to suit the needs of the audience. In any school there will be mathematicians in the audience so it is important that any graphs and tables are used appropriately. It may be worth asking a member of the Maths department to take a look in advance. It is important not to present just lots of averages as this can make any staffroom glaze over. The same can be true of a large number of graphs. This is where the regular insertion of pupil quotes can hold teachers' interest and makes the data real.

CASE STUDY 5.2: ANALYSING G&T CLASSROOM PRACTICE

Aim of the questionnaire

On an annual basis a G&T co-ordinator surveys the students on the G&T register with the aim of identifying good classroom practice and sharing it with the staff. The students range from Year 7–13.

Completing the questionnaire

The G&T co-ordinator takes the pupils out of lessons to complete the questionnaire so that she can talk them through the rationale for completing it. This includes explaining that they must not name individual teachers and they must bear in mind what it is possible for her to implement, so, for example, there isn't much point in the students requesting major curriculum changes which were beyond her control. The co-ordinator has found that having the students in a classroom all together has led to some very similar responses to the questionnaire. She also has tried sending the questionnaires out to home addresses but has had very few responses when this method has been used.

Questionnaire

1. What makes a good lesson?
2. What helps you enjoy learning?
3. Do you have opportunities to study independently?

    Often   Sometimes   Never

4. Explain
5. Do you find the work challenging?

    Often   Sometimes   Never

6. Examples
7. What would an appropriately challenging lesson be like?
8. What could teachers/school do to help you enhance your learning?

Analysing the results

The results of the questionnaire were not analysed in a heavily quantitative fashion. Instead the G&T co-ordinator highlighted comments from the students which should develop teaching and learning. To aid analysis the co-ordinator initially focused on students in Year 7 and 9, comparing their responses.

Question 1: What makes a good lesson?

Year 7 responses:
* Kinaesthetic activities (overwhelming – all but one of the student responses listed some kind of practical activity as their best lesson)
* Working in pupil-selected groups

Year 9 responses:
* Information posters
* Leaving the classroom
* Being stretched
* Role playing
* Group work leading to class discussion
* Choosing what I do in lessons
* Independent learning/research

Question 5: Do you find the work challenging?

Year 7
Two said 'Mostly'; ten said 'Sometimes'
Comments:
* Most subjects aren't challenging
* Only Maths is hard
* I'd like lessons to be a bit more challenging, but not a lot

Year 9
Four said 'Mostly'; one said 'Sometimes'; two said 'Never'
Comments:
* It depends whether we're in sets

Presenting the results

The G&T co-ordinator presented the results at a staff meeting. The first year this caused some controversy as the question 'What stops you from enjoying learning?' was included so the G&T co-ordinator changed her process of presenting the results. Instead, the results were made available on the network and staff were told this at a staff briefing and encouraged to look at them. The G&T co-ordinator is also planning to set up a G&T teaching and learning group on a voluntary basis, and will use the results of the questionnaires to inform their discussions as they aim to share good practice.

Review your learning

Questionnaires are an effective way of gathering data from a large number of pupils. They are rarely used by schools to evaluate the quality of teaching and learning because they depend heavily on the opinion of the pupils. Instead, they tend to be used for gathering factual information on wider school issues.

Managing the use of questionnaires can be very time-consuming and, without careful design, their use can waste time. It is also important to consider how they will be completed so the data gathered is valid.

The use of e-learning technology to manage questionnaires has the potential to revolutionize their use and the implementation of Virtual Learning Environments will mean it is quicker and easier to poll large number of pupils on a range of issues.

Key questions

To decide if your use of questionnaires is effective ask yourself the following questions:

1. Do you know what you are looking for?
2. Do you have a sample which will give a variety of views?
3. When and how will the questionnaires be completed?
4. Can you easily analyse the data?
5. How will you present the findings to staff?
6. Can you use the evidence to clearly identify areas for development?

CHAPTER 6

Pupils conducting lesson observations

The basics

Lesson observations have already been discussed in Chapter 2 but one growth area in school self-evaluation is the role that pupils can play in the process. For some schools this would appear a unusual idea and hence will be covered here in its own chapter.

There is no doubt that the subject of pupils observing lessons is a very controversial one for both teachers and parents. In schools where there is not an accepted culture of openness in teachers observing each other the idea of the pupils observing lessons could potentially cause considerable stress and conflict. There will be also be some parents who feel that their children should be receiving, not observing, lessons and could consider that their child observing lessons is a waste of time.

If pupils' views on the quality of the teaching they receive are being acknowledged via pupil focus groups and questionnaires then it would seem the next stage would be for pupils to observe lessons. In many ways it could be argued that they are the ones in the best position to tell teachers and leaders which lessons are the most effective. It could be considered quite arrogant for teachers to assume that they know what lessons are most interesting, the most memorable or include the best explanations. Pupils are the actual consumers and can explain the reality rather than the assumption.

In many other fields the views of children are being considered with great care. There is a growing acknowledgement that young people are becoming ever more sophisticated consumers with worthwhile and valuable opinions. So it becomes logical that schools should take their views into account too.

Identifying your starting point

1. Are there any current occasions where students observe lessons at your school?
2. How do staff respond to these situations?
3. How would culture of observations in your school affect the implementation of using students as observers?
4. How would your school benefit from students observing lessons?

The detail
Implementing a system of student as observers

Before any wide-scale or formal use of student as observers is implemented, consider the following factors:

- The purpose of the observation
- The accepted behaviour of the student observers
- What training the students require
- Whether the students will be participating in the lesson as well as observing
- How they will record the observation
- What feedback the students will give

What are the purposes of pupil observation?

Students observing lessons could have three main purposes in self-evaluation. These are helping individual teachers to improve their practice through research; providing feedback on candidates for teaching positions and as part of a school self-evaluation system.

When teachers are researching their own practice with the aim of developing their craft as a classroom practitioner, there can often be benefits to explaining this to the students engaged in the learning. Pupils are often fascinated by the idea that teachers wish to improve their teaching and will be only too willing to provide feedback. A common way of achieving this is through questionnaires (see Case Study 5.2). Focus groups can also be used, as can individual interviews with children. However both these scenarios require the students to think back to their memories of the lesson rather than reflecting on the teaching at the time. A more immediate response would be given by a student observing what is going on in the lesson at the time. If teachers ask students to observe their own practice this can be an effective way of students getting used to the idea of conducting observations. Feedback from the teacher can also be useful in breaking down the anxiety that many teachers would have when students observe their lessons.

The second scenario in which it is likely to see students observe a teacher is when teachers are giving a lesson as part of the interview process. Many schools ask teachers to deliver a lesson during an interview day and will then ask pupils for their opinions on the lesson. Including pupils in such discussions can make them feel part of the process rather than it just being done to them. Once the initial step of asking pupils their opinion has been taken it is not a huge jump to train pupils to sit alongside the teacher or governor observer and observe the lesson, rather than participating in it. When teachers at interview undergo this process and have a positive experience through being successfully appointed, this can provide the catalyst for students to participate in observations as part of school self-evaluation.

The third scenario is where students observe as part of a self-evaluation process. The pupil will take on the same role as a teacher observing a lesson. For many schools this can be a considerable change in culture but there is no doubt that schools that have begun this process have become richer learning environments as a result of it.

If the purpose of observation is this last scenario, selection of teachers becomes a considerable issue. In many schools that have developed student observation teachers have volunteered for the process. Therefore, the main focus of the self-evaluation is more about providing CPD for individual teachers, rather than contributing data to a whole school evaluation system, even though it could feed into this. It would take a real culture change in many schools for student observations to become an expected norm in which all teachers participate, though some schools may aspire to this and some have even made considerable progress on the journey towards it.

CASE STUDY 6.1: INFORMAL PUPIL OBSERVATION FEEDBACK

One school always asked prospective teachers to deliver a lesson to pupils as part of the interview process. Prior to the lesson it was explained to the pupils that this was an interview lesson and there was a possibility that the teacher would be working at the school next year. It was always explained to the pupils that the school was looking for the best possible teachers as that was what the pupils deserved. At the same time the pupils were told that at the end of the lesson they would be asked what they thought of the lesson.

At least one teacher from the school always observed the lesson. Following the lesson the pupils as a group were asked for their feedback on the lesson. The questions included:

1. Did they enjoy the lesson?
2. Were they stretched?
3. Was the teacher their school's type of person?
4. Would they like the teacher to teach them next year?

The pupils always gave very thoughtful and intelligent responses whatever their age. It was generally found that pupils' feedback matched that of the teacher observer and the pupils views were given as feedback to candidates who were not appointed. In one year the school conducted a large number of interviews due to school expansion and many of the pupils were in three or four interview observations. It was noticeable how they began to expect to give feedback and, as result, the feedback became ever more thoughtful.

Developing a protocol

All schools have behaviour policies and students recognize what acceptable levels of behaviour are. In any school some students' behaviour does not meet that level of expectation but there is an accepted norm of how pupils relate to each other and their teachers.

Students taking on the role of observers can be unsettling to both students and teachers as it can turn the relationship between pupil and teacher upside down. For this reason it is very important for a protocol of the students' behaviour to be clearly explained. This is likely to be different, depending on if the student is also participating in the lesson.

In many situations there will be three parts to the protocol. The first will be how the student behaves in the lesson, the second is the type of feedback given and the third is how the student reacts towards the teacher in future interactions. At the root of each of these points is clarity of the student's role with respect to the teacher. This can be covered by the idea that everybody can improve their skills, whether that skill is teaching or learning. The student is helping either the teacher improve their craft or the school to appoint the best teachers or the school to improve as a whole. However, at the same time, the student still has to do what the teacher tells them to do and the student must give the teacher the normal degree of respect.

During the lesson, whether they are participating in the lesson or purely acting as an observer, the student should not behave in any way which stops other people in the class from learning. In terms of the feedback it is normally made clear that the comments given must not be personal. Students must also realize that the observation is a one-off activity and that in interactions with the teacher they should show the normal level of respect towards the teacher.

Many teachers are concerned that, if pupils observe their teaching, in future they will try to use this as a way of usurping their authority. However, schools have found that, if the protocol and behavioural expectations are made clear to the pupils, this is not case. It also accepted that not all the students are capable of helping to observe lessons and that taking this role is a considerable privilege and responsibility.

PAUSE AND REFLECT

- How could you encourage staff to ask for the views of their students to improve their practice?
- How can you gather the views of students upon interview lessons?
- Could student observation be used within your observation process?
- How would you expect students to behave if they are acting as observers?

Selecting and training pupils as observers

One of the ways of showing students that acting as an observer is a significant privilege is to invest time and energy in their selection and training. The first thing is to decide how the student observers will be chosen. The schools that have successfully implemented such schemes have begun with a small number of students. Some schools have suggested to their school council that this should be part of their role. This has the secondary benefit of enhancing school councils. Other schools have asked students to apply to become observers and application forms have been completed and then interviews held.

Finally, some schools have linked student observers to one particular subject so it becomes akin to a subject prefect role. Most schools who are developing students as observers have been eager to stress that it should not be seen as just a role for the most able students, but it should be open to all students regardless of their intelligence, providing they have the maturity for the task.

Observation training tends to be in two stages and in many ways should mirror that which teachers receive. Part of the training is generally conducted outside of lessons. This could be where a lead teacher needs to explain to the students what the purpose of the observation is and also works with the pupils to determine what a good lesson is like. The second part of the training is more practical – students try observing a lesson and share their feedback with a teacher. Some schools using students as observers always make sure they observe the lesson with another adult.

SAMPLE ACTIVITIES FOR STUDENTS AS OBSERVERS TRAINING SESSION

Task A: Students think of a successful lesson they have recently enjoyed and describe why it was successful.

Task B: Students brainstorm what makes lessons successful.

Task C: Students consider what the role of an observer is.

Task D: Students consider how they should behave during a lesson observation. The students write their own guidelines of how they will behave.

Task E: Students watch recordings of lessons and describe whether they are successful and why.

The key to many of these tasks is students analysing and then justifying their opinions. These are skills which are obviously very useful for them in many spheres of their learning.

With many projects in schools one of the key issues is sustainability and part of this is in developing the roles of the students who act as observers. One way that this can be done is for students to take on the role of training future student observers, which ensures the long-term future of the project.

CASE STUDY 6.2: MAKING LEARNING BETTER

At the George Mitchell Community College in London, a system of student observation, known as 'Making Learning Better', has been implemented, where students have been trained to conduct regular lesson observations and give feedback to teachers.

Student observers are known as Learning Consultants and work specifically within one subject area. Students are encouraged to complete an application form if they wish to take on the role. It is suggested that the subject they apply for should be one they enjoy as this gives them a real motivation to help improve the teaching and learning in this area. The school has worked hard to ensure that the role of Learning Consultant is open to all abilities of students. The Curriculum Leader chooses the Learning Consultants with the aim that they can work productively with the students from the start.

Students are trained for the role in the belief that students are receiving transferable skills which will aid their learning as a whole. The training focuses on skills including questioning, problem-solving, critical thinking, observation and interpersonal skills, including feedback.

The Learning Consultant will receive a copy of the teacher's lesson plan a couple of days before the observation and after the lesson they give feedback to the teacher on the learning they have observed.

To try to make the programme as accessible as possible to all students the observation strategy is distilled down to two questions: did all the class members enjoy the lesson? Did learning take place? This simplicity of language is key to the accessibility of scheme. There is also an aim that teachers will regularly ask their classes these questions, whether an observation is occurring or not.

Learning Consultants have a wider role beyond observing the lessons. They are expected to provide training and induction for new Learning Consultants so the system is sustainable. They attend some staff meetings so they are aware of the new Teaching and Learning initiatives the school is developing and to give their own views on how these can be most effective. They are involved in working groups alongside teachers to develop school policies on teaching and learning. They participate in appointing new staff to the school.

Adapted with permission from an article in Learning and Teaching Update or Secondary Headship, published by Optimus Education www.optimus-education.co.uk

Figure 6.1: A pro forma for a student observing a lesson

Student Observation Sheet	
Name of student:	Name of teacher:
Date:	Subject:
Year group:	
Did the class member enjoy the lesson? How do you know?	Yes / No
Did learning happen? How do you know?	Yes / No

A more detailed lesson observation form could be produced by amending the one shown as Figure 2.2 in Chapter 2. This observation form would be more suitable for more sophisticated students.

Figure 6.2: A pro forma for a student observing a lesson

Student Observation Sheet	
Name of student:	Name of teacher:
Date:	Subject:
Year group:	
What made this lesson successful?	How could be it even better?

Recording the observation

The main function of the recording is as an aide-mémoire for the student so that they can remember what was particularly good about the lesson and how it can be improved further. It is important that the student's recording method does not disturb the lesson in progress. This would suggest a written method.

The observation pro forma needs to be quite simple so that the student is concentrating on the lesson rather than the piece of recording. It does need to be age specific, as a Year 6 pupil would probably require something different from a Year 13 student who is also a governor. The pro forma should be designed with the aim of scaffolding the student's thoughts and aiding their observation. One of the simplest ways of addressing this issue is to consider two key points about the lesson: did the pupils enjoy the lesson? And did learning take place? At the simplest level a student observer could just tick their response to these two questions and, if they were able to, they could explain why.

CASE STUDY 6.3: TEACHERS AND STUDENT CO-PLANNING

The Central Foundation Girls School in London has developed the Teacher and Student Co-Planning initiative over the last five years. A student teacher was struggling to teach a lesson. One of the girls in the group packed up really slowly at the end of the lesson and then asked the teacher if she was ok and offered to help the teacher plan the next lesson. The next lesson went so well that the student teacher was inspired and described the incident to other staff at the school. The school recognized that this was a great opportunity for developing teaching and learning at the school and considered how they could formalize a process where pupils could help trainee teachers develop their teaching.

Each student teacher is paired up with two pupils whom they do not teach. The pupils meet with the teacher to plan a lesson, they then observe the lesson before giving both written and oral feedback.

The school undertakes a very rigorous selection process. The Head of Year, in consultation with form tutors, is asked to recommend a range of pupils to undertake the initiative. Initially they undertook a rigorous interview conducted by a Deputy Head. As the initiative has developed the pupils now assist with the interviewing process.

Pupils who are selected undertake a full day's training to prepare them for the role. The first component of the training looked at two things. The first was why is the project being done? The second was what makes a good lesson, teacher and learner? They had to pick an exemplar lesson for reciprocity, resilience, resourcefulness, reflection, learning styles and suggest how each of those could be improved. Once this had been established the school wanted to give the pupils an idea of what it felt like to teach a lesson and then receive feedback. The pupils had to prepare a 15-minute lesson which they gave to the other pupils. The other pupils then had to give feedback. This was developed to consider what good feedback is and also how you use language to made the process more constructive. The final component of the training was the co-planning section. Teachers were invited to bring topics and work with pupils to plan exciting lessons. This had an added advantage in that teachers who participated in this element of the training often wanted to join the programme when they realized the quality of help the pupils could give. At the end of the training the pupils had to sign a contract outlining the expectations of them and the importance of confidentiality.

Initially the pupils used an observation sheet which subject mentors usually completed for student teachers. The pupils then developed this observation pro forma into a format that they felt was more suitable. (This is included as Appendix 6.1.)

The pupils arrange to meet the teacher the lunchtime after the lesson to present their feedback. They always give oral and written feedback.

Initially this programme was established to support trainee teachers but existing teachers at the school have begun to volunteer for the programme. The school generally now uses pupils in Years 7–10. Year 11 pupils would like to stay involved but the school feels they need to be in their lessons.

There is no doubt that this programme has given the pupils an opportunity to develop a wide range of skills, including interviewing, observation and providing feedback. It has also given student teachers a different perspective on their lessons and, more surprisingly, greater confidence in their classroom practice.

> **PAUSE AND REFLECT**
>
> - How will students be selected as observers?
> - What type of training will be given to the student observers?
> - Will the observers complete an observation form? If so, what will the form include?

Observers or participants
A decision needs to be made as to whether the students are participating in the lesson or purely observing the lesson. There are advantages and disadvantages to either system.

If the student is participating in the lesson, then they will be in the best position to comment on how effective the learning has been and whether they have enjoyed the lesson. This is the situation that was described in Case Study 6.1. Though, in some ways, there is a debate as to whether the student is observing the lesson or just giving feedback on the lesson they have participated in. It is unlikely that a student could participate in the lesson and still complete an observation form, so the feedback is reliant on the student's memory. This probably does work best with a teacher whom the student has not met before, as in the interview scenario, otherwise the student's memories will be affected by previous lessons with that teacher and the feedback may not be on that lesson alone.

If the student is purely observing the lesson they will be paying attention to the lesson in a different way and they will be judging the other students' enjoyment of the lesson, rather than their own. The student also has to make the same judgement as a teacher as to whether learning has occurred, which can be a considerable challenge for any observer. The teacher can be concerned that the student observer does not disrupt the lesson by interacting with the other students. Lastly, the student will be missing a lesson of their own to conduct the observation which some teachers and parents might not support.

> **CASE STUDY 6.4: STUDENTS AS LEARNING PARTNERS (SALP)**
>
> Launceston College in Cornwall has developed its student voice programme to enable students to provide feedback on the quality of teaching and learning. The school felt that, as industry constantly asks customers to observe, monitor and feedback on

their products, they should give their customers, the students, the same opportunity.

The first step was to sell this concept to both the students and the teachers. The students attended a training event outside of school with Specialist Schools and Academy Trust which greatly enthused the students. With teachers, the idea was to start off with a small group of volunteer teachers and then to create a positive momentum so that it could be rolled out among larger sections of the college.

The college recognized that not all students would be 'up to the job'. They selected the observers from their pool of tutor group reps, already known at this college as student learning reps.

The school created a protocol based on the acronym SHORT (Sensitivity, Honesty, Openness, Respect and Trust) which all student observers had to agree to. This was included in a written contract that student observers had to sign prior to any observation. Also contained within the contract was an agreement that all observation details and feedback would remain confidential, that the teacher would agree the date, and time and focus of the observation with the student in advance and that the student would seek the agreement of their normal class teacher so they could absent themselves to observe the lesson.

The student received training with students from other schools on how they would conduct their lesson observations. They began the day by producing a mind map on the importance of students in the role of learning. They were then introduced to the ideas included within SHORT. The students looked at how they could give feedback by brainstorming positive and negative phrases which could not, or should not, be given as observation feedback. They were also given a page of vocabulary to help in this process. The final part of the training process was to watch a video recording of an actual lesson. The students were given a focus and they completed observation sheets on their thoughts on the lesson. Lastly, the students had to present their feedback to the group and other members of the group then commented on its appropriateness.

The teachers who participated in the process were volunteers. Each teacher worked with two student observers. The student observers were from different year groups and were students who were not in the teachers' usual classes.

> For any observation, the student and teacher work through a six-point programme. The teacher sets a focus for the observation. The student and teacher then meet to discuss the focus and agree a date and time for the observation. The student signs up to the SHORT protocol, including the confidentiality agreement. The observation takes place and the student completes an observation form on the lesson. The student feeds back to the teacher in a manner agreed by the teacher. This could be a verbal or a written piece of feedback. Finally, the teacher and student agree a time for a subsequent observation.
>
> *Adapted with permission from an article in Learning and Teaching Update or Secondary Headship, published by Optimus Education www.optimus-education.co.uk*

Giving feedback

If the observation has any value feedback must be given to either the teacher or the school. The latter is only likely to occur in an interview scenario. Teachers can find it very difficult to give feedback to fellow teachers following a lesson observation so this is likely to be a difficult process.

It is important to spend time training students on how to give feedback and modelling appropriate language. The careful design of an appropriate lesson observation form can aid this process. Where the teacher is researching their own practice it can be slightly more straightforward as the teacher can question the observer about what they thought of specific points about the lesson. This can also be mimicked to a certain extent by the teacher and student agreeing a focus before the lesson.

A second method which can support the teacher is allowing the teacher to choose how they wish to be given the feedback. So a teacher could, for instance, request written feedback. This situation could occur if the teacher felt that the lesson was not to the required standard and written feedback would spare their feelings.

PAUSE AND REFLECT

- Will students be participants or solely observers of the lesson?
- Will the observation have a focus?
- How will the lesson feedback be managed?

Review your learning
Student voice is an area of considerable growth within schools and, if schools are going to fully get to grips with the agenda, students must have the opportunity to provide feedback on the quality of teaching they receive and the learning they participate in.

If a school is going to implement a student observation system of any kind it must be planned with extreme care. Students must be carefully selected and then undergo some kind of training programme so that the observation can be as effective as possible. It is not appropriate to just expect students to be able to observe a lesson.

A suitable protocol must be established so that students recognize how they should behave during an observation and also so that teachers know what to expect from the observation. The school needs to carefully consider what record will be kept of the observation and how these will aid the student with their observation.

There is no doubt that feedback could be the most contentious element of any student observation process. So the school must carefully plan how this will be delivered and train students in this. The aim must be that teacher practice improves and that barriers are removed between the teacher and student, rather than new ones being created.

Key questions
To decide if you could use student observations in your school ask yourself the following questions:

1. Do you have a group of teachers who would wish to participate in such a process?
2. Would students wish to observe lessons?
3. Is there the capacity in the school to provide the appropriate training for students?
4. How would student observation add to other evaluation systems in the school?
5. How could you make the system you introduce sustainable?

Acknowledgements
Many thanks to Joy Morgan of the Central Foundation Girl's School for explaining the TASC programme.

CHAPTER 7

Analysing statistical data

The basics

The final self-evaluation tool considered in this book is data. For many people data analysis would be the first thing to come into their mind when the term self-evaluation is used. In a bid to promote the other tools of self-evaluation, data is being considered last here.

There is such a range of data currently available in schools. This includes data which is given to schools by outside agencies such as the DCSF or Local Authorities and also data sets which schools pay for, such as those available from NFER. In addition, data sets are compiled in school on a wide range of features. With so many columns of figures it can be difficult to know which ones to start with. Indeed, one key decision for school leaders is to choose which to use with their staff. A Middle Leader may then reduce this data further as they work with their teachers. Somebody researching a specific issue may use only one or two data sets and thus the choice becomes even more important.

Once the data has been identified, it needs to be used. Many educationalists find the analysis of data a frightening beast and in many ways understanding data is a little like learning a foreign language. To begin with it is very daunting, as you just do not know where to begin but, once you learn a few bits, you rapidly begin to make other connections and understand more and more. Whole books have been written on data and this chapter does not intend to replicate such tomes. Instead, a little like the 'learn a language in an hour' materials available in the shops, this chapter aims to give you enough knowledge to demystify the subject and get you started on some basic conversations. Just as when getting around a foreign city you do not need to understand the pluperfect subjunctive of the language of the that city, to conduct your own data self-analysis you do not need to know how Contextual Value Added figures are calculated.

One development in many schools concerns the frequency that data should be studied. Teachers have become used to an annual cycle of data review, whether for performance management or in departmental or class reviews. There is now a growing trend to study data at various points during the school year so this information can be used to inform both the teaching and learning in the school and also to develop other systems. This type of analysis is known as 'tracking' and a number of systems will also be included.

This chapter should be particularly suitable for Senior Leaders who have lost confidence in their use of data, possibly after having being baffled by a School Improvement Partner seemingly using a different set of data every minute in a two-hour meeting. It should provide enough information for an existing Senior Leader to begin some analysis or for a prospective Senior Leader to have some ideas with which to tackle an interview task. Middle Leaders will be able to use the ideas to evaluate the work of their team and a practitioner can use the ideas to evaluate a piece of research they have completed.

Identifying your starting point

1. What school data sets do you currently feel confident in using?
2. Which data sets does your school currently evaluate?
3. Which aspect of your school do you wish to evaluate?
4. What data is available to help with this?

The detail

Planning data analysis

Due to many colleagues' insecurities regarding the use of data, it is crucial that analysis is carefully considered in advance. Addressing the following factors should achieve this:

- The aim of the data analysis
- The pupils or people to whom the data refers
- The data set which is used

- The type of analysis that will be conducted
- The frequency with which the analysis occurs

What is aim of the data analysis?
For many Senior Leaders the aim of their data analysis to discover how effectively their school is performing. The automatic thought for many is the wide range of assessment data that is available. These could include standard benchmarking scores such as the percentage of pupils achieving level 4 at the end of Key Stage Two, reaching level 5 at the end of the Key Stage 3, five GCSE at grade C and above or five GCSE at grade C and above, including English and Mathematics.

Another measure of how well the school is performing could be linked to the results of lesson observations and this could include the percentage of the lessons at various OFSTED grades. It is not uncommon to find schools that have favourable intakes and achieve excellent examination grades yet, when the teaching is examined, it is not up to the same standard. This has certainly been identified by OFSTED when schools have received an Outstanding grade overall, reflecting the quality of the attainment of the pupils, but have not reached Outstanding for the quality of teaching and learning in the school.

Many educationalists would consider another important reflection of a school's performance is whether the pupils in the school feel safe and enjoy their learning. These are statistics which maybe acquired from questionnaires such as a pupil attitudes survey.

For many teachers the effectiveness of a school may be considered the standards of behaviour in that school and whether pupils are effectively dealt with when their behaviour falls below that expected. Data on this issue may be that held within the School Information Management System.

Middle Leaders with a curriculum responsibility will often be looking at similar statistics, except those will be relevant to their subject area. One of the interesting things for Middle Leaders is whether the comparison they are making is between their own performance in previous years or is a comparison with other subject areas. A Middle Leader may also be looking at the performance of different teachers. They could also remove the personalities from the equation, when looking at data, and consider the outcomes of different grouping arrangements.

Middle Leaders with pastoral responsibilities, Heads of Year, will be studying performance data relevant to their year group. If the cohort is still within the school the comparison may look at other year groups still in the school. If the cohort has left the school the study may be related to other previous cohorts. The Head of Year may also be studying the performance of different curriculum areas to discover if some are outperforming others.

A teacher researcher is likely to have a specific research question which determines the required data. Perhaps they are studying how the different gender groups progress in their group relative to the style of teaching used. They may be using two different styles of teaching with two groups to see if this impacts upon their attainment and if one style is more effective than another.

PAUSE AND REFLECT

- What is your key question or questions?
- What data sets in schools are relevant to this question?
- Which do you feel happiest working with?
- What measures would you be expected to use by your School Improvement Partner, your Headteacher or your research co-ordinator?

CASE STUDY 7.1: HEAD OF FACULTY STUDYING PERFORMANCE OVER TIME

A Head of Faculty was looking at how their faculty had performed over a five-period year for a line-management meeting with their Headteacher. The simplest measure to look at was the percentage of pupils achieving Grade C and above.

Year 1	Year 2	Year 3	Year 4	Year 5
38%	40%	60%	62%	55%

The immediate conclusion was that the faculty performance had followed a rising trend and then fallen away in the most recent year.

The Head of Faculty knew they could put a positive spin on this by using a three-year rolling average. This is where the mean average is taken of three years. Then the oldest year is removed and more recent one is included, and so on.

Rolling Average 1: (38+40+60) / 3 = 46%
Rolling Average 2: (40+60+62) / 3 = 54%
Rolling Average 3: (60+62+55) / 3 = 59%

On this analysis the Head of Faculty could claim tell their Headteacher that the faculty was still showing a rising trend.

The Head of Faculty was interested to see what explanations could be given for the dip in performance as the teachers in the faculty had not changed. They looked at the gender balance in the different year groups.

Year 1: 80 boys/70 girls
Year 2: 78 boys/71 girls
Year 3: 74 boys/78 girls
Year 4: 71 boys/76 girls
Year 5: 85 boys/66 girls

This showed that the results for Year 4 had risen as the number of girls relative to boys had also risen. However in Year 5 there were vastly more boys in the year group than the girls.

Who does the data refer to?
The starting point for most data evaluation is academic performance data. This often refers to pupils who are no longer in the school. You could be studying Key Stage 2 data on Year 6 pupils who have now moved to the secondary school, it could be GCSE results of Year 11 pupils or A-level performance of Year 13 students.

There is a growing trend to look at the academic performance of students still in the school. Leaders have had experience of this when looking at either Key Stage 2 or Key Stage 3 results. As exams have become more modular in basis, schools now receive regular data on the academic performance of young people still in the school. This could include core Science GCSE results at the end of Year 10 or AS module results at the end of Year 12.

Other measures which could be considered will often refer to young people who are still on roll. This could range from anything from pastoral data to data for the school travel plan.

It is important to consider if the issue you are investigating relates to all the pupils in the school or to a particular key stage, year group or even vertical house grouping arrangement. Data can often lack meaning without a useful point of reference to make a comparison with. Do you wish to compare the data between different groups within a school? This is often the suitable approach if the study is of in-house data sets or could be suitable if you are comparing the relative performance of a certain group within the school against the rest of the cohort. A good example of this is gender performance analysis, which is touched upon in Case Study 7.1. You may wish to make a comparison between pupils in your school and national measures, in which case you need to ensure that data is available.

Of course the other kind of comparison you could make is one over time. This generally compares one year group with another and again is one that is looked at in Case Study 7.1.

PAUSE AND REFLECT

- Which group of pupils are you researching?
- Do you need the data of all pupils or are you using some kind of sample?
- What are you comparing the population or sample with?

Which data set will be used?

This is often the hardest question to answer and this section will give a brief overview of some of the different types of data that are available in school.

Academic performance data

The most obvious type of academic performance data is how children have achieved in external examinations. At Key Stage 2 and 3 this will be the number of pupils who have attained certain levels and at GCSE or A-level it will the numbers of pupils who have attained certain grades. It is often more useful to use percentages, especially with large cohorts of pupils, and as sizes of cohorts change, this makes analysis more straightforward. If you are working with small cohorts you may wish to use pupil number as, for example, the 10 per cent of pupils who only got a level 3 in their Mathematics Key Stage 2 assessment may refer to only two pupils in a small primary school class of 20.

It can be difficult to compare percentages of pupils over nine different grades at GCSE, A* to Ungraded and even more at Key Stage 3, when you include B, N and absent in the mix. Instead schools tend to look at the percentage of pupils who have achieved certain thresholds of performance. There are some thresholds which are expected performance of pupils at certain points so you could be considering the percentage of pupils who have reached level 4 and above at Key Stage 2, level 5 and above at Key Stage 3 or grade C and above at Key Stage 4.

Another threshold analysis could be related to a certain group of pupils. You could be looking at the performance of more able pupils, so be studying the percentage of level 5 at Key Stage 2, the percentage of pupils who achieve a level 7 or 8 at Key Stage 3 or the percentage of pupils who achieve three A/A* grades at GCSE. A school could also be looking at its inclusion performance so the percentage of pupils who achieve level 3 and above at Key Stage 3 or grade G and above at GCSE.

Most people realize there is something inherently unfair about looking at a pupil's performance at a certain point and using this to make judgements about teaching or learning or the effectiveness of a school, as this takes no account of the amount of progress a pupil makes. For instance, it could be argued that the child who starts secondary school with Key Stage 2 level 3 in Mathematics and reaches grade B at GCSE has made more progress than a child with a Key Stage 2 level 5 in Mathematics who reaches grade A at GCSE. It is for this reason that value added measures are increasingly used. Value added basically considers the pupil's starting point in terms of attainment and the attainment they reach and gives this progress a score.

Many value added measures work on the basis of a residual. What this means is that the pupil's starting point is considered, for example their Key Stage 2 scores, and a calculation is made which determines what grades they are most likely to achieve for GCSE performance. If the pupil achieves above this grade we say they have a positive value added or a positive residual. If a pupil achieves below this grade we say they have a negative value added or a negative residual. The leading statistical group in this area is the Fischer Family Trust. They calculate the pupil's expected performance against national data. To try to make the data more reliable, a researcher can look at the value added measures for different groups of schools, i.e. the schools that are high performing, low performing or for all schools.

There are other groups which also calculate value added data. Rather than using the child's performance in a national test such as Key Stage 2 or Key Stage 3 SATS, these groups use their own tests as a starting point. One group of such tests are PIPs, MIDYis, YELLIS and ALLIS operated by Centre for Evaluation and Monitoring. The NFER group also uses Cognitive Ability Test Scores for benchmarking. The interesting thing to note about both of these banks of tests is they consider the ability of the child as a starting point rather than an external test which should take account of the quality of the pupil's teaching.

In terms of complexity, above Value Added data is Contextual Value Added data or CVA. This data also takes account of social factors such as ethnicity, free school meals and other social groupings to determine what performance children should expect to achieve. Again, the Fischer Family Trust is a leading supplier of such data.

Non-academic data

There is a host of other sources of data in school. Some of these will be calculated by all schools and hence will allow schools to compare themselves against other schools. Good examples would be data on attendance, free school meals, ethnicity, turbulence (the percentage of pupils who begin at the school and remain at the school), pupils with statements and exclusion data.

There will be other sources of data which Local Authorities will gather which will enable schools to compare themselves with other schools locally. One example would be travel plan data which may be useful for certain building plans.

There is also the wide range of data which schools collect themselves from their own measure. Pastoral data is a good example, where schools will have their own method of scoring good and poor behaviour of pupils and keeping a record of this.

CASE STUDY 7.2: TEACHER PERFORMANCE

A Senior Leadership Team was concerned about the performance of their Mathematics faculty which appeared to be below that of other faculties. This was based on the percentage of pupils achieving grade C in Mathematics which was lower than for Science, English and Humanities subjects. The Head of Faculty explained that there was not an issue as students were making as good progress as in any other faculty, it was just that the pupils in Mathematics started from a lower base point. The Head of Faculty also claimed that the teaching in some of the feeder primary schools was not as effective as for other core subjects. Some Senior Leaders believed that a number of teachers were not producing the results that they should be. The Mathematics faculty organized the pupils into six hierarchical sets. When the raw GCSE pass rate was considered, the results were as expected, in that the results were in a hierarchical order.

Set	Percentage of pupils who attained grade C and above
Set 1:	100%
Set 2:	97%
Set 3:	75%
Set 4:	45%
Set 5:	40%
Set 6:	0%

A Senior Leader then worked with the Head of Faculty to look at the YELLIS residual performance. YELLIS calculated the pupil's expected performance at GCSE and gave this a decimal number. The pupil's actual GCSE grade was also turned into a whole number and this was taken away from the pupil's YELLIS expected performance to leave a negative number if the pupil had achieved less than expected or a positive number if their achievement was better than expected. These numbers were then totalled for each group.

Set	Total of YELLIS residuals
Set 1:	0.8
Set 2:	2.6
Set 3:	-.07
Set 4:	-3.5
Set 5:	1.6
Set 6:	4.2

These figures indicate that two teachers, the teachers of set 2 and set 6, were achieving very good value added data, whereas for the teacher of set 4 the opposite was true. The Senior Leader was perhaps right is saying that there may be issues in the quality of teaching and learning for this group. When the residuals were totalled for all six Mathematics groups it was found that these were consistent with the performance of other faculties. So the Head of Faculty may have also been right in his assumptions here too.

What analysis will be conducted?
The analysis can be conducted in-house or external calculations can be used. In terms of attainment or progress, even though there are situations where a school can use YELLIS or CATs data to provide some significant analysis, in the current climate it is best for a state school to use Raise Online for its starting point in statistical analysis. How to analyse Raise Online could be a book in itself due to the sheer volume of data which is included. The best advice for educationalists is to gain confidence in using a small number of measures provided. So a secondary school leader may look at CVA for all Key Stage 4 subjects and use this to make comparisons to try to ascertain which curriculum areas are strong within the school and which appear weak. The school leader may also look at the CVA of specific groups, such as boys, girls, children with free school meals or children who speak English as a second language, and then compare the CVA of these groups with pupils in similar schools. These few analysis points can provide a rich source of analysis.

One of the dangers for any educationalist is that another person with a broader knowledge of data may then seek to bamboozle with more data measures. In such circumstances it can be best to listen to such arguments but then to return to the measures that the school leader is confident in understanding and ask for conclusions to be drawn solely from these.

It is important to look at analysis over time and see if there are any obvious trends. What no school leader wishes to see is a declining trend where results appear to be getting worse. There is little point in hiding such findings, however. Instead it is important to try to develop an understanding of why such trends are occurring. At this point it may be worthwhile comparing such data with that which has been developed from other methods of self-evaluation for triangulation. It is also important for Middle Leaders and classroom teachers to conduct their own analysis, whether this is through a performance-management system or departmental audit.

CASE STUDY 7.3: DEPARTMENT MINI-SEFS

It can be useful for Middle Leaders to conduct their own analysis of the performance of their own subject area. In many schools this is known as a mini-SEF process. A pro forma is created which mimics the style of the SEF and Middle Leaders have to find the relevant data, place it in the appropriate locations and conduct their own self-analysis.

Two extracts of a department SEF are shown in Figures 7.1 and 7.2. An example of a complete department SEF is shown in Appendix 7.1. Figure 7.1 asks the Middle Leader to look at a new number of data sets and then use these to make judgements about the performance of the department. To be able to make such judgements, the Middle Leader really needs to compare the data from their department against other subject areas in the school or to Raise Online to make comparison against other schools.

In Figure 7.2 the Middle Leader needs to begin the analysing the performance of individual teachers within the department by using value added residual data as in Case Study 7.2. The Middle Leader is also asked to suggest reasons for these performances.

Figure 7.1: *A mini-SEF extract*

Aspect	Outstanding	Good	Satisfactory	Improvement required	Evidence (suggestions given)
Learners' achievements and standards in their work					SAT results CVA scores
Progress of the most able relative your subject in all schools nationally					Level 7/8 average at well over 45% in last three years.

Figure 7.2: *Extract from a department mini-SEF*

Record the residual scores for each of the staff in your department who taught Year 11 last year

Staff member	Residual	Comment
Suggestions below		
EG 1	−7.34	Difficult low attaining group. 16 of the 27 got their worst or joint worst GCSE result here. One achieved his best.
EG2	−2.06	Took over a very low achieving set at Christmas.
EG3	+3.5	Pleasing result. 68% got their best or joint best GCSE grade in this subject result here. 31% of the group got grade C or above.

How often should the analysis take place?

Typically in schools data analysis has often been done at the end of the year after the pupils have completed their year's study. This may have been done in the autumn term. With the publication of the Autumn Package or Panda reports, the forerunners to Raise Online, such analysis may have been even later. In the case of analysing school's own measures, such as data on pupil behaviour, this has often been completed in the summer term.

The problem with both of these scenarios is that the pupils have moved on a year and may even have left the school, so it is unlikely that the analysis can have an impact on the pupils at the appropriate time.

It is for this reason that many schools are now studying the academic performance or the behaviour of pupils as an ongoing process during the academic year. This type of analysis is often called tracking.

A tracking system allows individual teachers, Heads of Department, Heads of Year and SLTs to monitor the academic progress of every pupil more closely. Tracking systems need to be based on consistent and accurate data so that teachers are able to intervene with pupils and give specific and practical advice on how they can improve. Tracking systems should also involve parents, Teaching Assistants and subsequent teachers in the process.

Tracking is part of a cycle that many teachers are already implementing in an informal or formal way. Schools often track pupils' effort or behaviour over the year or Key Stage through the reports or monitoring that they communicate to parents. Schools also track the number of behavioural incidents that pupils are involved in over the year or the rewards that they gather. In addition, some departments are often working in isolation to develop their own tracking systems. This often occurs in Science and Mathematics departments which have implemented a modular examination systems and the Middle Leader will analyse how the pupils have performed on such periodical assessments. However, a whole school system will enable good practice to be more widespread and will enable all teachers to adapt their planning to suit the needs of their pupils. Tracking also enables the school to praise those pupils who are being successful at their target level and to know which need extra support or intervention.

In many schools introducing a more consistent tracking system is a whole school priority. Many schools are anxious that the process should not be onerous for any teacher. Most schools will already reporting on pupil progress twice a year in the form of academic reports where teachers are tasked to give National Curriculum levels or GCSE grades for pupils and identify how they are achieving relative to their KS2, KS3 or KS4 targets. The best tracking systems aim to provide this information alongside pupils' target levels in an easily understandable format.

CASE STUDY 7.4: TRACKING PUPIL PROGRESS AT KEY STAGE 3

The following case study considers how one school developed its own tracking system at Key Stage 3. The school used a traffic light system so the tracking system could be visually analysed and numerically analysed.

The process

A department spreadsheet is created by the data manager which has the pupils' assessments for the end of KS2 as the start point and the Fischer Family Trust Band D Predictions for pupils' end of KS3 assessment.

Pupil targets (including a, b & c descriptors) are calculated for the first five school reporting points – two in year 7, two in year 8 and two in year 9 – by the data manager. This information is then given to class teachers for them to record in their mark book (electronic or paper) and shared with pupils.

Each teacher reports on pupil progress twice a year. The system will then compare attainment to the pupil targets and will judge whether each pupil is:

- A cause for real concern due to underperformance (red)
- Potentially unlikely to meet their end of year target (orange)
- On course to meet their year target (green)
- Exceeding their target for the year based on current work rate (blue)

Individual class teachers will be expected to:

Share targets with pupils, along with information on how to achieve them in the relevant assessment objectives for their subject, e.g. English reading, writing, speaking and listening EN2 EN3 EN1

- Use intervention methods to support pupils failing to meet their target level, e.g. revision of skills, additional tasks at home, additional focus in class and creation of resources
- Use assessment for learning techniques, e.g. formative marking, level ladders, etc. to show pupils what it is they need to do to improve

Heads of Subject/Department will be expected to:

- Monitor that the above is being done by all teachers in their subject
- Keep a record of the targets for all pupils in their subject, along with information issued by the data manager regarding progress towards the targets, which should be available for the Headteacher/Deputy Headteacher, department consultants and OFSTED to see at any time
- Use the tracking information to inform department meeting discussions regarding pupil progress, schemes of work, lesson planning, etc.
- Support department teachers in applying the necessary intervention strategies to ensure pupil progress
- Oversee department practice on target setting and review with pupils. If a department system does not currently exist one should be introduced and all members of the department supported in its use

Heads of Year are expected to:

Oversee and be fully apprised of the progress of their year group, through access to academic overview data. At tracking points the Heads of Year should contact parents of pupils who have a significant number of subjects in which they are underperforming. Printouts of the data will enable Heads of Year to identify these pupils effectively.

Review your learning

The analysis of data must lie at the heart of any self-evaluation process but it is important to resist the temptation of only considering statistical data in self-evaluation. There are many people involved in education who appear to consider only data. This criticism is made by many educationalists of the person above them in the hierarchy, whether it be a teacher describing their Head of Department or a Headteacher discussing their School Improvement Partner. It is therefore important to use data not in isolation but to consider it alongside other forms of self-evaluation.

It is easy to become lost in the massive quantity of data available and all educationalists looking at self-evaluation should be self-disciplined in using a smaller group of data sets, especially if they wish to discuss their findings with others who may not have such confidence.

As with any type of self-evaluation it is important to begin with a clear aim in mind and then carefully consider what type of data is the most appropriate to help investigate this aim.

It is easy to be scared of data and the trick to building one's confidence is to begin with a small amount and practise analysing and evaluating that, just as it easier to begin speaking a foreign language with a few simple phrases.

Key questions

To decide if your use of data is effective ask yourself the following questions:

1   Do you know what you are looking for?

2   Have you decided which pupils or area of the school you are studying?

3   Have you identified the most appropriate data sets for your aim?

4   How will you analyse the data?

5   When will the analysis be conducted?

PART 2

SELF-EVALUATION IN PRACTICE

CHAPTER 8

Teaching and learning review systems

The basics

A background to evaluation was presented in Chapter 1 and a range of reasons were presented for why schools wish to evaluate. These included providing evidence required for writing the SEF or determining the most appropriate CPD required to move a school forwards.

In the first section of this book the focus has been on the study of a variety of tools which schools can use to evaluate aspects of their progress. The final chapters will consider how these tools can be used together, rather than in isolation. Drawing conclusions based on the evidence from one tool can cause inaccuracy and is also a potential source of conflict in the staffroom as teachers can feel that one 'snapshot' is unrepresentative of their own work and that of their subject or year group.

Until fairly recently the system of evaluation in many schools would have consisted purely of a timetable of observations of teaching staff, as explained in Chapter 2. However, there is an obvious inherent danger in using a single data source. Many schools recognized this and began to consider examination data, along with the observations findings. This was beginning a process of triangulation.

The concept of triangulation has already been mentioned on a number of occasions. Triangulation is where a number of self-evaluation tools are used and the findings of each are considered to see if there is a consistency in the evidence that is gathered. These conclusions are likely to be more accurate and representative of the work in school and, as a result, will be more acceptable to staff.

The process of evaluating the teaching and learning in a whole school can often be a challenging one as so many individuals contribute to the overall results. However, if a school is going to progress, this evaluation is vital. Many school leaders have the aim of trying to develop a system of evaluation which breaks this down into something more manageable. There are generally two main styles of systems. The first is where the work of particular subject areas is evaluated. This could be studying the effectiveness of a strand of learning in a primary school, such as numeracy or literacy. In a secondary school it could be looking at the provision from one department or faculty. In some schools these have been called faculty reviews, department maintenance checks or even mini OFSTEDs. An alternative strategy can be to consider how a particular year group or key stage is performing. In schools where vertical arrangements of learning, such as houses, have been created, these could also be evaluated.

Once school leaders have decided how the school will be subdivided to facilitate evaluation, the next stage is to consider which tools of evaluation will be used and how they will be integrated to ensure there is triangulation of evidence. It is also important to consider the timescale over which these evaluations will occur and even how they will feed into writing the SEF or a CPD framework.

Identifying your starting point

- What self-evaluation system is currently used in your school?
- What is the main purpose of the system?
- Does the system provide the evidence that the school requires?
- What are the main strengths of the current system?
- What are the major weaknesses of the current system?

The detail
Organizing a successful review system
Review systems can quickly become complex entities for many reasons. They can involve a wide range of people, both those conducting the review and those being reviewed. There can also be a number of reviews to undertake if the whole school is being studied. This obviously takes time, so the reviewers have to be careful to create a system that is sustainable. These factors mean that review systems must be carefully organized. When developing a review system the following points should be addressed:

- The reason the evidence is being gathered
- The sections into which the school will be divided
- The self-evaluation tools used
- The people involved, both reviewers and reviewees
- The frequency of the reviews
- How the data will be analysed
- How the information will be shared

Why is the evidence being gathered?
There will be a multitude of reasons that review systems are being developed. In English maintained schools today the most likely reason for review systems to be used is to provide evidence for the SEF. Therefore it is worth considering for which section of the SEF you are trying to gather evidence so that system does provide appropriate evidence.

A second reason for designing review systems is to analyse what CPD is required to move the school forwards and how effectively recent CPD has been integrated into the day to day practices of the school. A third reason for developing review systems is if a school has a new leadership team and they wish to understand where the school lies on its journey of development.

What sections will the school be divided into?
There are some Senior Leaders who do not divide the school into sections when implementing a school evaluation system but instead choose to use a week or two weeks to review the work of the whole school. In effect, the school is operating its own OFSTED procedure. This system has more in common with the previous incarnations of inspection procedures than the current shorter models. The immediate benefit is that the conclusions will be drawn across the whole school.

The most obvious drawback is that it is a massive undertaking for the school. It is likely that the leadership team would have to solely concentrate on this task and would not be able to achieve anything else in this period of time. If there were any incidents in this time many schools would lack the capacity to deal with them. It also puts a considerable strain on teaching staff and could lead to the post-OFSTED dip that many teachers will remember. This is where teachers work so hard in the run-up to an inspection, and during it, that they can take their foot off the pedal, so to speak, after the inspection and the result is the school coasts along for a while.

Many schools instead will review their school along subject lines by reviewing the work of each over a cycle of time. This sectioning tends to work well for larger subject areas, whether numeracy in a primary school or Mathematics in a secondary school, as this will look at the work of a range of teachers. Where subject reviews are less effective is for the one-teacher department such as Music, Drama or Religious Studies. In such circumstances leaders may group them together to form subject areas such as Performing Arts, (Music, Art and Drama)or Humanities (Geography, History and Religious Studies.) It does help to group subjects together in this way as the review is not then an intensive examination of the work of one teacher but it can make the forming of consistent conclusions more challenging.

An alternate system could be to review the work of a year group or a key stage. This is likely to more manageable in a small or medium-size primary school than in a large secondary school, as again it will look at the work of a small group of teachers. Schools which have formed schools within a school, such as a vertical house system in particular, may use this as the unit they look at. In comparison to the previous example, this is more effective if there is a core group of teachers working with the house.

However the school is divided, it is often most effective to use division where a Middle Leader is responsible for the work and the teachers in that section of the school, be they a Head of Department, Key Stage Co-ordinator or Head of House. There is then somebody to feedback to who can take on board development points and work to implement them.

PAUSE AND REFLECT

- What is the specific reason for organizing a school review system?
- What evidence is required?
- What subdivision of your school is most appropriate to review?
- Does this include all sections of the teaching community in your school?

Which self-evaluations tools will be used?

It is unlikely that you would develop a review system which uses all six of the self-evaluations tools explained in Part 1 as this would produce an unmanageable and unwieldy review system. The quantity of data could also make forming conclusions challenging. Most teaching and learning review systems have lesson observations at their heart and then select two more tools for triangulation purposes.

It is often a good idea to use a tool which considers the pupils' opinions of their learning. A school could run a consistent focus group for each subject area or key stage or could use a pupil questionnaire. The obvious advantage of using a focus group is that views of the pupils can be explored and specific comments from pupils can be developed. In comparison, a questionnaire allows the views of a greater number of pupils to be considered so could be considered more statistically valid.

A third category of self-evaluation tool could be one which looks at the work the pupils produce. In terms of developing teaching and learning this could be a work scrutiny, as this considers the progress of the pupils over a longer period of time than a single lesson observation. Equally, the examination results or teacher assessments could also be used to compare the progress between different subjects or even between different teachers in one subject area.

CASE STUDY 8.1: DEPARTMENT MAINTENANCE CHECK

A small secondary school entitled their review system 'The Department Maintenance Check'. This name was chosen to make the process sound more supportive and less judgemental. The rationale for the check was it would be the vehicle for the Senior Leadership Team to monitor the standards of teaching and learning across the school, study the impact of whole school initiatives and identify training needs. The results could feed into the school SEF, performance management and CPD strategic planning.

The school was divided into eight departments, each with a Middle Leader responsible for standards within the department and performance-management of the teachers within the department. These were English, Expressive Arts, Humanities, Science, Languages, Mathematics, PE and Technology.

The departmental maintenance check would use three self-evaluation tools:

- A lesson observation of each member of teaching staff. The observation could be one of the performance management observations, so in that year the HOD will only have to conduct one other observation to meet the performance-management requirements.
- A book check. This would look at the work of six pupils within a year – two each of high, middle and low ability –

and would ensure there is a book, folder or artefacts from each teacher, with the exception of PE.
- A pupil focus group of a different year group from the work scrutiny. The sample, as for the book check, would consist of six pupils from a year with the same ability range as the book check.

The cycle would be to monitor each department over the period of five terms. With there being a maximum of four teachers in any one department, there are a maximum six tasks (four observations, one book check and one focus group). This means generally each member of the SLT will have one task for each maintenance check. In addition, if the School Business Manager conducted some of the focus groups, then one member of the SLT would not have a task.

Time	Department	Number of Teachers
Winter Half Term 1	Technology	3
Winter Half Term 2	English	3
Spring Term	Mathematics/Lang	3/2
Summer Term	Science	4
Winter Half Term 1	Humanities	4
Winter Half Term 2	Expressive Arts	3
Spring Term	PE	3
Summer Term	Cycle continues	

The process would be managed by one member of the Senior Leadership Team taking responsibility for leading the department maintenance check. At a Senior Leadership Team meeting the roles within the check would be divided up and there would then be a two-week window to complete the check. The SLT meeting immediately after this window would be a maintenance check analysis meeting where the evidence from the check would be analysed and appropriate conclusions drawn. The lead person from the SLT for the check would feedback to the Head of Department first and then to the department.

In the appendixes a number of pro formas are included which support the process:

Appendix 2.2: Lesson observation pro forma

Appendix 3.1: Work scrutiny pro forma

Appendix 8.1: Maintenance check schedule

Appendix 8.2: Feedback sheets to share with HODs

Appendix 8.3: Pupil focus group questions

Who will be involved?
It is likely that in many schools it will be members of the Senior Leadership Team who are acting as the reviewers in the process. In schools where there is a link governor for each subject area they could be asked to participate in the process. Schools that are receiving support from Local Authorities may ask LA consultants to also assist in the process.

Some schools have set up more innovative leadership system. For instance, in one school there was a team of Advanced Skills Teachers who were more senior than Heads of Faculty. They were responsible for developing teaching and learning in the school and, hence, as a team conducted subject reviews.

Some schools have delegated these reviews to the Middle Leader responsible for the department with the mandate that they use their evidence from performance management and their own monitoring to review the work of the department. In some ways this mirrors the new OFSTED arrangements where inspectors ask the Senior Leadership Team to make judgements on the school and then they monitor these judgements. In the same way, in this example Middle Leaders make judgements and these are scrutinized by Senior Leaders.

The important thing within such systems is that there is a vehicle for the Middle Leader to collate the evidence to be easily discussed and then scrutinized by Senior Leaders. Some schools have called such document mini-SEFs. An example is presented as Figure 8.1 overleaf.

Figure 8.1: *Department mini-SEF*

Section A

Aspect	Outstanding	Good	Satisfactory	Improvement required	Evidence (Suggestions given)
Learners' achievements and standards in their work					Classroom observations SAT results CVA scores
Quality of teaching and learning					Classroom observations
Effectiveness of self-evaluation procedures					Classroom observations. Subject reviews. Quality file.
Improvement since the last subject review					Classroom observations. Refer to review findings.
Progress of the least able relative to your subject in all schools nationally					Difficult to assess as now the very least able do not do subject x as an option.
Progress of the most able relative to your subject in all schools nationally					Level 7/8 average at well over 45% in last three years.
Contribution of the subject to the development of learners' sporting and healthy lifestyle skills					New KS3 Schemes of work reflect subjects commitment to specialist status of school by x.

Use lessons judgments by Senior Team and the head of subject to draw conclusions about the quality of teaching.

Section B
GCSE A*–C %

	All	Boys	Girls	CVA KS2–4 see RAISEonline	Significantly above or below national average using RAISEonline
2008					
2009					
2010					
Three-year average					

GCSE A*/A %

2008 estimated	2009	2010

KS3

	Level 5+		Level 6+		Level 7+	
	School	National	School	National	School	National
2008						
2009						
2010 estimated						
Boy/Girl achievement						

Section C
In relation to similar schools how well do you think students in your subject are progressing?

Outstanding	
Better than most	
Average	
Not as good as many	
Poorly	

In relation to other subjects in this school how well do you think your students are progressing?

Outstanding	
Better than most	
Average	
Not as good as many	
Poorly	

Staff performance
Record the residual scores for each of the staff in your department who taught Year 11 last year.

Staff member	Residual	Comment
Suggestions below		
EG 1	−7.34	Difficult low attaining group. 16 of the 27 got their worst or joint worst result here. One achieved his best.
EG2	−2.06	Took over a very low achieving set at Christmas.
EG3	+3.5	Pleasing result. 68% got their best or joint best result here. 31% of the 65 got level 7 or 8.

TEACHING AND LEARNING REVIEW SYSTEMS 111

Areas for improvement (maximum of three)

Area	Reason
Suggestions below	
Ensuring best practice is embedded within the whole department. Emphasis on pace within lessons and challenge.	Classroom observations show best practice is not embedded across the department.

Please complete a department report of no more than one side of A4 which gives any other information you wish to include.

Use the following headings:

- Departmental successes and recent initiatives (supported with evidence)
- Extra-curricular contribution of the department to the life of the school
- Barriers to departmental improvement and the department's efforts to overcome them

The frequency of the reviews

One of the biggest challenges with establishing any evaluation system is to make sure it is manageable. It can be very tempting to aim to review every subject area over the course of an academic year and, while this is an admirable intention, it may prove impossible. For the school described in Case Study 8.1, the whole school review is divided into eight subject areas and to complete this in one academic year would effectively mean a subject area is being evaluated every month. This was felt to be unsustainable. The school in Case Study 8.1 actually felt the five-term cycle was a considerable challenge and sought to find a speedier way to conduct the process.

> ### CASE STUDY 8.2: ADAPTING THE DEPARTMENT MAINTENANCE CHECK
>
> The school recently was graded as Outstanding as OFSTED so wished to free up Senior Leadership capacity from monitoring and evaluation to look at further development. The school decided to move away from evaluating the school on subject guidelines and to move to a more whole school review system. The new review system consisted of the same components, lesson observations, work scrutiny and a pupil focus group, but these would now be conducted by a range of staff rather than members of the Senior Leadership Team only.
>
> *Learning walks/blink reviews*
>
> Rather than using formal lesson observations the school wished to develop the idea of blink review, which was looked at in Case Study 2.3. Once a month for a double lesson, two members of the SLT would conduct a learning walk, remaining in classrooms for approximately ten minutes.

Work scrutiny

Once a term in an SLT meeting, a work scrutiny check of one particular year group would be conducted. This could consist of four pupils, one of above average ability, two average ability pupils and one of below average ability. The pro forma shown as Figure 3.1 would be used. This would be then collated so Middle Leaders could receive detailed feedback on the four pupils just for their subject. It would also be intended to highlight any strengths or weaknesses which could be communicated to the whole staff.

Pupil focus groups

To develop the role of the year leader, rather than conducting a subject related focus group, the year leader could conduct a more general focus group of six pupils in their year. These would be conducted once a half term and hence all five year groups would be monitored by midway through the summer term. The year leader would be provided with administrative support to take notes of the focus group so that the year leader could concentrate on asking the questions.

How will the data be analysed?

With any method of review system it is likely that reviewers will begin the process with a series of preconceptions about the area of the school that is being reviewed. It is important when the data is being analysed that any conclusions are drawn from the evidence from the review and not from any preconceptions.

The data from each part of the review process should be compared. The reviewer is looking first for any consistent points that are highlighted by more than one tool in the review. Secondly, the reviewer should be looking for any inconsistencies between the tools. An example of this would be the teacher who delivers a particular style of lesson, perhaps one heavily dependent on ICT while the pupil focus group and work scrutiny show no evidence of the use of ICT in teaching.

How will the information be shared?

Any type of review process is stressful for the teachers whose work is being analysed so it is important that the information is shared sensitively and the teachers are thanked for allowing the review to take place.

It is often useful for the main reviewer to go through the information that has been gathered with the line manager of the subject or key stage. Where such staff are highly competent they can also be involved in either the data analysis and the feedback or in both. As with lesson observation feedback, it is good practice to highlight areas of strengths and points for development. All the pro formas should be shared with the line manager and they should be given copies of the pro formas for their own records.

Once this has been completed, the teachers within the area also have to be given feedback on the overall process. On many occasions it can be useful for the main reviewer to present the feedback to the teachers with the line manager.

CASE STUDY 8.3: SUBJECT SELF-EVALUATION AND SUBJECT REVIEW PROCEDURES

Rationale

The purpose of Subject Reviews is to raise standards. They are carried out by the Senior Team and mirror the pattern of short notice OFSTED inspections. The Vice Principal should draw up the schedule for subject reviews in the preceding summer term of each year. No subject will be reviewed at the same time of year on two successive occasions. Each review should last no longer than three days. Any complaint should be made to the Senior Team link. If no agreement is achieved, the complaint will be discussed with the Principal.

Start of the review

Lead Teachers, with three days' notice, should submit the Quality File and any Department Handbook containing the most up to date Departmental mini-SEF at the beginning of the review and will be invited to report on:

- An evaluation of current pupil attainment and progress using data provided by the most up to date tracking point and an indication of how likely pupils are to meet FFTD predictions.
- An evaluation of the impact of the contribution of each member of the team, including LRAs, TAs and technicians, in line with their performance-management targets (action and progress made).
- An evaluation of the impact of the department's Improvement Plan targets on students' standards of achievement (KS3 and 4) (action and progress made).

- Examples of the department's contribution to the Every Child Matters agenda, such as European exchanges, school productions, trips, sports fixtures, etc. and where they can be observed.
- Examples of PLTSs.
- Examples of innovative use of ICT.
- The impact on students' standards of achievement (KS3 and 4) of the targets, strategies and processes agreed at the previous review (action and progress made), if applicable.

The report is given to the SLT for reading, prior to the subsequent meeting, at the start of the review. At this meeting, and based upon the contents of the report, the ST Link and the Subject Leader agree the following:

- The focus of the observations. This should normally include KS3 and 4 classes, as well as a range of abilities. Teachers should not be reviewed with the same age and ability class observed in any previous review.
- The composition of the student focus group (the Lead Teacher could select 8–10 students of differing ages, gender and ability).
- The process for the evaluation of students' work, which should include book checks during lesson observations.

Other relevant documentation:

- The student focus group questions
- The lesson observation documentation

Lesson observation protocol

Observers should ensure:

1. Feedback to staff should be given within 48 working hours of an observation
2. Observed staff know they have a right to appeal to their line manager against a conclusion
3. Documentation is given to the member of staff observed and the Lead Teacher after an observation

Staff being observed should:

1. Submit a lesson plan for the observer

2   Be prepared to show mark books, student targets and tracking evidence if required

3   Supply information about the SEN and Gifted and Talented requirements of particular students if required

Pupil work scrutiny protocol

The member of the Senior Team carrying out the scrutiny should ensure the following:

1   A selection of no more than 12 books or folders across the ability range to be requested

2   Staff be given 24 hours' notice before collection

3   Books and folders should be returned within 48 hours of collection

4   A copy of conclusions be given to the Lead Teacher

Student focus group protocol

The member of Senior Team carrying out the review should ensure the following:

1   A selection of no more than ten students be assembled

2   Students be given 24 hours' notice

3   The group should take place at a lunch time and students allowed an early or late lunch if required

4   Comments made in the group remain anonymous

5   Students should not be allowed to make personal comments about staff

6   Completed documentation is copied to the subject leader

Quality files

Maintained by every subject leader, the file should contain the following:

- Departmental mini-SEFs
- Current and recent improvement plans
- Results of examinations and teacher assessments for last three years
- Current and recent tracking information

- Current Subject Review Action Plan
- Outcomes of recent external consultancies, i.e. Notes of Visit from the LA consultants

The file may contain other performance data that the subject leader considers useful for evaluation the performance of the department.

End of the review

At the end of the review the subject leader will take part in a discussion of all the evidence and an action plan for improvement will be agreed. A member of the SLT will write this up. All documentation is to be kept in the SLT Subject files, except for one copy of the summary sheet, which is kept in the Principal's SEF evidence files, and a copy given to the Lead Teacher.

Senior Team links

Each permanent member of the Senior Team oversees subjects and is responsible for liaison on the following:

- Performance
- Improvement planning
- Staffing and personnel
- Training
- Timetabling
- Subject reviews, action plans and interim reports
- Trips
- Equal opportunities
- Curriculum
- Effective use of department capitation
- Bidding for development funds
- Parents
- Links with governors, business partners and the Parents' Association

Other relevant matters may also be discussed from time to time.

Senior Team/Lead Teacher meetings

- One meeting, early in the autumn term, should focus on examination performance, the departmental SEF, progress towards the improvement plan

- One meeting in the summer term should focus on planning for the next academic year
- Other meetings should provide Lead Teachers with an opportunity to communicate ideas and concerns to the Senior Team

Review your learning

In today's schools conducting reviews is an important part of the monitoring and evaluation function that all Senior Leaders are expected to do. Depending on different schools' priorities and their current stage in development their review system will be different. The review systems in a school recently judged Outstanding are likely to be very different from a school trying to emerge from special measure with a new Headteacher in post.

It is crucial that any review systems are carefully planned, both in an operations sense of how they will be conducted, and from a strategic perspective of where the evidence gathered will be utilized. It is also necessary to ensure that review system is sustainable and can be conducted at the dates agreed.

Review systems in many cases will be conducted by the Senior Leadership team so it requires each member of the team to be in support of the process otherwise slippage will occur and agreed cycles will fail.

Key questions

To decide if your use of review systems is effective ask yourself the following questions:

1. How does the review system dovetail with other monitoring and evaluation processes?
2. Does the review provide the evidence you require?
3. Is the cycle of review maintained?
4. Do Middle Leaders value the process and gain from it?
5. Does the Senior Leadership support the process?

CHAPTER 9

Self-evaluation of Continuous Professional Development

The basics

There is a direct link between Continuous Professional Development and school self-evaluation and that is in being reflective. It is likely that if you are trying to develop a culture of self-evaluation in your school you will already have put Continuous Professional Development at the heart of your school or you intend to do so.

It is important that the evaluation of CPD is not seen a self-contained exercise, separate from school self-evaluation but, instead, the two processes should feed into each other, use the same tools and the same evidence and, in turn, support each other.

In recent years the funding settlement for schools has been less generous than in previous years. It has not been uncommon to hear of schools where the staffing bill increased by 5 per cent due to rising salary costs, yet the funding settlement has only increased by 3 per cent. This ignores the effects of other increasing costs, such as utility bills, which cause as many problems in schools as they do in private homes. Many expect funding settlements in the future to become ever tighter, due to the effect of the economic downturn on the public purse.

At such times of financial belt-tightening many Headteachers can be under pressure to find economies while still allowing their school to progress. The easiest solution to this conundrum is a tightening of belts, setting a budget with the middle name of 'prudence', informing staff that there will no additional expenditure and constantly searching for cost centres where savings can be made. We can all think of occasions when this has happened in the schools we have worked in. I can still remember beginning one autumn term early in my career with financial restrictions echoing in my ears, best summarized by the CPD co-ordinator announcing that there would be no external courses for any colleagues except those new to post. At the time this was seen as real tightening of the purse strings. I can remember thinking that, although this was an obvious area of saving, surely the one thing that we should not cut in a school is our investment in improving the education of pupils. This appeared as illogical to me at the time as a major company cutting its research and development budget in times of hardship. If an institution wishes to climb out of a slump the one thing it needs to do in search of a new market or a new product is to improve the company's viability.

Some schools will have considered how they can provide a more personalized CPD provision in the most cost-effective fashion. Senior Leaders may have been encouraged to look at CPD provision which is of low cost, such as bringing CPD provision in-house and using the expertise of staff within the school. Individual teachers may have looked for CPD opportunities that have limited cost to the school, such as those funded by external agencies or those which the teacher studies in their own time. Indeed, the CPD co-ordinator in your school may have the aim of developing an ethos where colleagues are encouraged to take control of increasing their personal effectiveness. This can ensure that continual improvement for staff is a reality and not just a buzzword.

A second reaction to such budget tightening would be the school working to ensure that the CPD that is delivered in school or accessed by the school is most effective. This could be by ensuring it is actually needed in the first place and that, when it occurs, it delivers improvement to the school.

Identifying your starting point

1   Does your school have a system in place to develop CPD?
2   What self-evaluation tools are used to evaluate CPD?
3   Who is responsible for evaluating CPD?
4   Is school self-evaluation linked to CPD evaluation?

The detail
Developing a system of CPD evaluation
There are a number of points which need to be considered for a school to develop effective and efficient systems to evaluate CPD:

- The schools understanding of what CPD is
- The points where CPD can be evaluated
- The link between CPD and school self-evaluation
- The most appropriate tools to use at each point in the CPD cycle

What is Continuous Professional Development?
Unfortunately, if you ask teachers in some schools what CPD is, their answer is still likely to be either that it is a one-day external course or it is when an outside trainer has delivered a session during one of the five teacher days that schools can place during the academic year.

Many schools, especially those which have the investors in people accreditation, will take a much broader view of CPD and will seek to find regular opportunities during the school year to promote CPD activities. Schools will use meeting slot time for CPD. This could be a member of staff or an LA advisor delivering a session to the whole staff, it could be a number of staff providing a carousel of sessions in longer post-school slot, generally called twilight training. Schools may also provide training in time slotted for meetings which staff can opt into, according to what they feel is appropriate for their development. Schools will also encourage Middle Leaders to provide CPD opportunities during team meetings. CPD co-ordinators may seek to facilitate training via the Virtual Learning Environment which teachers can access in their own time. Some teachers will undertake courses in their own time. These could be academic studies towards Masters Qualifications or other such certificates. Many CPD co-ordinators are trying to develop peer observation as a means of CPD. These do share a common theme with one-day courses in that they are pre-planned CPD opportunities.

There are also all the opportunities for CPD that will arise as a result of developing a culture of reflection and self-evaluation. When teachers undertake any activity and then reflect on it, with the aim of improving their practice, they are developing their own CPD. Any feedback that is given from self-evaluation is an opportunity for CPD, especially if the views presented provide suggestions on how the colleague can make progress.

For these reasons the evaluation of CPD must not be perceived as a separate activity from school self-evaluation. Many school leaders would suggest that the evaluation of CPD should be integrated with school self-evaluation and each should inform the other. Indeed, some school leaders would move even further and suggest that school self-evaluation is, in fact, a form of CPD in itself if either the evaluator's practice or that of the teacher being evaluated improves as a result of the self-evaluation being conducted.

> **PAUSE AND REFLECT**
>
> - Can you list the CPD opportunities in your school this term?
> - What activities would your colleagues identify as CPD opportunities?
> - How has your practice improved as a result of conducting self-evaluation?
> - For those colleagues whose work has been evaluated, can you identify examples of their practice improving?

At what points can CPD be evaluated?
Educational researchers have identified different points at which CPD can be evaluated. For the purposes of this chapter this has been simplified to four points:

1. The first point is the reaction of the participant to the CPD that they have received. What was the participant's opinion of the training? Did they enjoy it? Were they stimulated by the input?

2. The second point is in relation to the participant's learning and how the CPD has impacted upon this. Has the participant gained knowledge, developed skills or had their attitudes changed as a result of the CPD?

After these two points the practice of the participant may not have changed and, as a result, it could be argued that the organization has not improved as a result of the CPD activity.

3. The third point is whether the participant begins to use the new knowledge or the skills that have been developed in their practice.

4. The fourth point of evaluating CPD in a school is whether the student learning outcomes have improved as a result of the CPD. Are the learners making more progress or has the learners' behaviour improved?

At the heart of all CPD is the hope that the student experience will improve as a result of CPD. However, this is a long term practice and

SELF-EVALUATION OF CONTINUOUS PROFESSIONAL DEVELOPMENT

it can often take time for this improvement to occur. For this reason it is still important to evaluate the quality of CPD at the four different points highlighted above.

The link between self-evaluation and CPD

The most appropriate CPD should arise as a result of the evidence of school self-evaluation. The appropriate CPD could have been implemented when self-evaluation identified a weakness in an individual's practice, in a group's practice or throughout the school. In this circumstance the self-evaluation may be considered as an audit of practice.

Following this audit it can be most appropriate to consider school self-evaluation and the points at which CPD can be evaluated as a cyclical relationship. The self-evaluation is the starting point. The participant then takes part in the CPD and forms a personal opinion on the CPD. The third point of the cycle is, what have the participants learnt from the CPD? The fourth point of the cycle is that the participants used this learning in their role. Fifth point of the cycle is that the students' learning outcomes have changed as a result of the CPD. This brings is back around to school self-evaluation.

Figure 9.1: *Integrated CPD/school self-evaluation cycle*

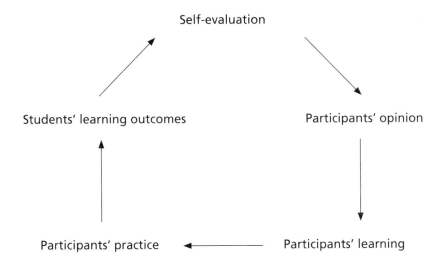

This cycle does not include the evaluation of the CPD. In some ways the CPD evaluation can be seen to sit at the centre of the cycle with spokes running out to the four points at which CPD can be evaluated. The impact which the CPD has had on the participant can be evaluated at each of the four points in time. The evidence from CPD self-evaluation should then feed into the school self-evaluation to identify whether the CPD has been effective and in this regard there are two key questions. The first is, have staff changed their practice? The second is, have the student learning outcomes changed?

Figure 9.2: *The relationship between CPD evaluation and self-evaluation.*

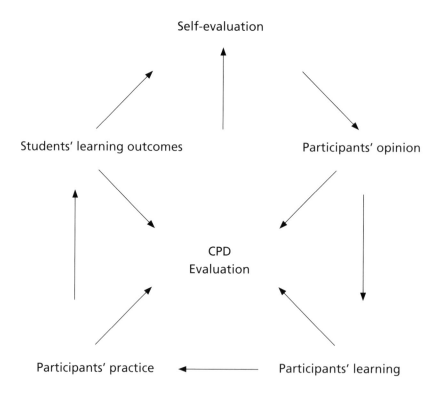

What tools can be used to evaluate CPD?

It is likely that different self-evaluation tools will be used to evaluate the effect or impact of the CPD on the participants' opinions, their learning, their practice and upon the student learning outcomes. These will also be done at varying lengths of time after the CPD has been delivered.

The impact of the CPD on the participants' opinions and their learning is likely occur immediately or soon after the CPD has been delivered. Often questionnaires will be seen as the most likely self-evaluation tool to gauge the impact upon the participants' opinions and their learning. However a focus group of participants' views could also

SELF-EVALUATION OF CONTINUOUS PROFESSIONAL DEVELOPMENT

provide a rich source of information. It is likely that CPD co-ordinators will not use this tool but, instead, will seek the views or verbal thoughts of participants after the CPD has been delivered. In some cases the participants will be only too eager to voice their comments if the CPD has been particularly poor or very impressive.

It is worth considering that, to truly measure the impact of the CPD on a participant, it is necessary to know what targets or objectives the CPD activity is designed to meet. If the CPD is personalized in the sense that one colleague is attending a course, the colleague should have raised their aims and objectives prior to attending the course and these will be used to select the course. Where the CPD is linked to performance management the aims and objectives should already have been recorded in the performance management targets. In the case where CPD is being delivered in a twilight session to the whole staff or a subsection of the staff, the CPD co-ordinator working with CPD leader should have identified the aims and objectives and communicated these to the participants.

CASE STUDY 9.1: EVALUATING CPD IMPACT THROUGH QUESTIONNAIRES

Context: A 3–18 independent school

Due to the age range of pupils the CPD co-ordinator was tasked with delivering a diverse range of CPD. The result of this was that, on the whole, CPD was heavily personalized and reliant on use of external courses. The CPD co-ordinator was working towards developing a culture of in-house CPD delivery but this was very much in its early stages. One of the most obvious signs of this change was the CPD co-ordinator publishing an in-house teaching and learning newsletter with the aim of sharing the best teaching and learning practice from teachers working at all age ranges.

Initially the CPD co-ordinator struggled to ensure that teachers completed post-CPD questionnaires so he wished to develop a system so that this was no longer so haphazard. There was also a need to carefully monitor the costs of CPD, especially as it was not only the course costs that were paid for by the CPD budget but also the travel costs.

A questionnaire was devised which was completed at various stages of the CPD process. To be booked onto a course the participant had to complete the first part of the questionnaire. They had to write down their aims and objectives for the course and also provide estimates of the travel costs. The CPD co-ordinator would book the course if it was deemed suitable and a copy of the questionnaire would be returned to the participant.

Once the participant had attended the course, they had to complete a second section of the questionnaire which asked for the participant's opinion of the course. They also had to state how suitable it had been in meeting the original aims and objectives. This was to evaluate the effect on learning. Lastly, the participant had to state how they would be prepared to share information from the course, possibly through departmental meetings, leading a staff meeting or by writing a short article for the teaching and learning newsletter. This was to measure the impact of the CPD on practice. On the reverse of the questionnaire was the travel expenses claim form. To have travel expenses refunded the participant had to complete the form.

After a period of time the CPD co-ordinator would return the questionnaire to the participant and ask if they had presented the information at a department meeting and, if so, to provide a copy of the minutes. Or he would encourage the participant to write an article for the in-house teaching and learning newsletter. In some cases the participant also made a short presentation to the whole staff. This allowed the CPD co-ordinator to measure the impact of the CPD on the participant's practice.

Generally, when the impact of the CPD upon the participant's practice or the student outcome is being evaluated, this can be linked in with self-evaluation tools that are being used to evaluate teaching and learning as a whole. This becomes even more straightforward when the CPD is a major strand of the school improvement plan and hence applies to all teachers.

If a lesson observation is being conducted the observer could have an observation focus to consider the impact of the CPD on the teacher's practice. The difficulty is in the observer being aware of what they are evaluating. However in the observation pro forma included earlier (Figure 2.2), a section of the form covering performance-management targets was completed by the teacher. These should also relate to the teacher's CPD and hence the observer would be able to comment on any impact seen. If the CPD has been a major strand of the school improvement plan these could be highlighted below Factors Promoting Effective Learning. The school which had designed Figure 2.2 may have been delivering CPD relating to Classroom Management, Differentiation and Assessment for Learning, as these are all highlighted in this pro forma.

If the impact of the CPD upon the student learning outcomes is being evaluated this could be seen through work scrutiny, pupil focus groups, pupil questionnaires and, hopefully, data. Again, this is easier if the CPD is an area that the whole staff is working upon, in which case the tool can be adapted to consider that area of CPD. If the school has been working upon assessment for learning as a CPD focus, in the work scrutiny pro forma there could be a column asking if the children know how well they have done in relation to learning objectives. There could be information explaining how they can improve their grade. In a pupil focus group questions pertinent to assessment for learning could be included. For example, in Case Study 4.4 there are three questions that link to assessment for learning. How often is your homework/classwork marked? What type of comments are the most/least helpful in improving your work? Do you know what grade your work would be if it were marked at KS3 SAT/GCSE level?

A similar process could be developed for pupil questionnaires. A good example would be that used by the teacher who is researching their own assessment in Case Study 5.2. The impact on attainment data is, of course, a longer term process. However, it should be expected that, if a school is successfully developing its assessment for learning practices, the data should be improved.

Where data analysis may be more straightforward is when the CPD is linked to the attainment of a particular group of students. Perhaps a whole school focus has been in developing the quality of writing as this is seen as a barrier to the progress of boys. If the CPD is successful it would be hoped that boys' attainment would improve. However it is also likely that girls' attainment would rise too.

Review your learning

For all CPD co-ordinators the evaluation of CPD should be seen as part of the process of the delivery of the CPD and not as a bolt-on afterwards. If the evaluation is integrated within the delivery of the CPD it is more likely to be completed. In addition, the act of participants reflecting on the CPD should increase its impact.

The evaluation of CPD should not be seen as separate from the school self-evaluation but should be considered as one component within the process and the link between the two should be recognized by the school leaders, particularly those who are responsible for writing improvement plans, whether at a departmental level or a whole school level.

If the evaluation of CPD is integrated within school self-evaluation, the tools used can be modified to ensure that CPD impact is evaluated. Not only does this make the process more manageable but it also means that all leaders are responsible for a culture of CPD within a school and it does not just fall on the shoulders of one individual.

Key questions

To decide if your CPD evaluation is effective ask yourself the following questions:

1. Is there a system for evaluating the impact of CPD on participant opinion and learning?
2. Is whole school evaluation used in CPD evaluation?
3. Are school evaluation tools modified to evaluate CPD?
4. Are all leaders evaluating the quality of CPD?

CHAPTER 10

Using self-evaluation to validate progress

The basics
The previous two chapters considered how self-evaluation tools can be used to monitor and evaluate the core provision of the school by looking at the quality of teaching and learning and by considering what impact CPD has on this.

This chapter will consider how self-evaluation can be used to validate a school's progress in a range of areas. A school could be seeking to evaluate its progress on a national priority, an in-school initiative or to gain data as a starting point for an externally validated award.

For many national priorities it is suggested that schools should use a cycle of review to determine the effectiveness of their provision. In the past good examples would have been the audits which the national strategies developed to look at literacy and numeracy in a school. The two more recent examples which will be covered in this section are evaluating extended services and the monitoring evaluation section of a specialist schools bid.

In previous chapters are case studies on how schools can use self-evaluation tools to study certain aspects of their provision, such as Case Study 5.3 which looks at how questionnaires could be used to analyse G&T classroom practice. The more in-depth example in this chapter is how a school can evaluate its behavioural management systems.

There is a vast range of external awards that schools can choose to work towards. When one walks into any school in the country, one can see evidence of this from the plaques on the walls of reception. Similarly, school letterheads often bear crests from different external bodies. There is accreditation which is aimed just at schools but there are also awards available to business in general, such as the Investors in the People award. In this chapter the NACE Challenge Award is considered.

This chapter is presented in a slightly different style from the earlier chapters in that 'The Detail' is presented solely through the case studies, without a commentary.

The detail
National priorities

> ### CASE STUDY 10.1: EVALUATING AN EXTENDED SCHOOL
>
> In the last three years, more and more schools have implemented the extended services core offer. Many school leaders will be very aware of the 2010 deadline that the government has set for all schools to meet this challenge. As an ever increasing number of schools have already met the core offer, this has been understood by OFSTED and the SEF has been altered to take account of this. Indeed in Section 1 of the SEF 'Characteristics of your school', part 1b asks the school to 'Please summarise briefly your distinctive aims and describe any special features of your school'. It includes the example, 'whether your school is an extended school and the rationale for the range of services you offer or make available through your school, in relation to the needs of pupils, their families and the community'. Further references to extended schools occur all the way through the SEF.
>
> Indeed, some Local Authorities have moved this on a stage further. The Directorate of Children's Services for the Isle of Wight Council have produced their own extended schools SEF with the rationale of allowing groups of schools 'to develop a coherent and evaluative commentary to support the decisions and progress made in the implementation and the sustaining of Extended Schools status'. It will be interesting to observe if other Local Authorities begin to take a similar view as the 2010 deadline approaches.
>
> As previously explained, the best self-evaluation draws carefully on a varied evidence base. It is not just personal opinion but,

instead, an analysis of varying sources of data. The most effective self-evaluation often consists of triangulation. This is where a number of methods of evaluation are used and consistent findings will be seen across different methods of evaluation. This case study will examine a variety of methods of self-evaluation, such as questionnaires, analysis of data, pupil focus groups, observations and work scrutiny, and consider what elements of the core offer they are most suited to gather evidence for.

Data analysis

The starting point for most schools in the self-evaluation process is to look at the available data of which there is currently masses. This inevitably begins with attainment data, though it is likely to be simplistic to link a rising trend in results with the commencement of your extended provision. It may, though, be possible for your data manager to compare the attainment of those pupils who have attended wraparound care with those who have not. You could also analyse the results of those children who may have attended study support classes with those who have not. However you may agree with Mike Welsh from Goddard Park Community Primary School that you cannot rely on SATs or GCSE data to monitor the progress of the extended school as 'there are too many variables involved in tracking back to improved family literacy and numeracy.' Instead, the data you are most likely to analyse is in terms of access to provision. How many children attend different elements of your extended provision? Which extra-curricular sessions are the most popular? When is wraparound care most used? Do you need a breakfast club every morning of the week? Likewise, you may do the same with looking at which parenting classes have been attended the most. Which agency referrals have been the most common? You may be able to record the number of hits on certain sections of your VLE which delivers aspects of the core offer. There will be a whole host of numerical data which you can analyse for your extended school which may raise questions as to whether some elements are needed, if they need greater marketing or whether you need to duplicate your provision due to take-up.

Questionnaires

Schools have conducted questionnaires of pupils' views for a considerable length of time. Your Local Authorities may even conduct and analyse pupil questionnaires themselves and compare one school with results of the county. It will be interesting to see in future years if these will be developed to include questions about the extended services provision. Questionnaires also form part of the data gathered by value added testing, such as YELLIS, and within them there are sections which consider the learning resources available in the home. As extended services become more sophisticated it is likely that pupils will be considering the resources that are available at school for their study support in this section. When you began researching your extended schools provision it is likely that you planned and then conducted a variety of questionnaires to try to ascertain which elements of the extended schools core offer were required in your community. You may have asked parents to complete questionnaires to determine the viability of wraparound care at you school. Pupils may have completed them to consider which activities would be most popular. You may even have asked staff to complete them to discover which learning issues required the most support in extra learning sessions. You may decide to repeat the same questionnaires with each group of stakeholders or you may develop a range of new ones.

Always test the questionnaire on a small sample of pupils or teachers in advance to ensure both the questions and nature of responses are clear.

Focus groups

You may decide that an area that needs evaluating is the quality of information that is provided to parents and carers so that they can support their children's learning. In which case the people that need to be involved is a group of parents, possibly with children at different stages of their school career, or you may decide you wish to focus on a certain age of pupil and thereby invite parents who have children in one year group to be involved. You could also conduct a focus group of pupils' views on specific support classes that they may have attended. You could also decide to conduct a focus group or interviews with a family group to discover how the elements of the extended school have linked together to support their children's or even the whole family's learning. You could cross-reference how the skills developed during parenting classes have enabled parents to support their children's progress.

Observations

It is then important to consider the different types of observations and how they can be used to help evaluate the extended school. A learning walk would provide evidence of the range of activities occurring on a single evening. This variety highlights the difficulty for the extended school co-ordinator in ensuring quality of provision.

You may have appointed additional staff to facilitate certain sessions, such as funding a health worker to deliver sessions to young mothers. It is just as important to observe this member of staff at work as any other in your school who delivers learning, not only to ensure consistent quality of provision but also for this colleague's CPD and to ensure they are performance-managed properly.

You may ask your PE staff to observe sports coaches at work, again to ensure good delivery of sessions but also to ensure the standards of safety you expect are being adhered to. It should have the additional benefit of being a professional development opportunity for the PE teacher, who may not specialize in that sport or who can apply the teaching techniques observed to their own practice. If your school is providing child care at the end or the beginning of the day this needs to be observed too, so that you can be sure the quality provided is that you would expect at your school and to check that safety is paramount.

There is no doubt that, without careful planning, observation could become onerous for any Senior Leadership Team. So, as has already been alluded to, it is important to involve a variety of staff. Additionally, it is also vital to ensure good recording tools are developed. You may find that you require very different observation pro formas from those you currently use for curriculum observations or you may develop a flexible resource which can be used through out the school. You also need to find a way of summarizing the observation data. It is perhaps unlikely that the OFSTED teaching criteria can be applied but identified strengths and areas of development of the sessions can be recorded. These can then be triangulated with other evidence that has been gathered.

It is important to remember there is the obvious difficulty of relying to heavily on this source of data and that they are just snapshots of a point in time. The strengths or weakness observed may be one-offs contrived by a mixture of circumstances.

Work scrutiny

There may not be a large source of written evidence from the extended school. It is likely that parenting classes will not have a written outcome unless the sessions have a second aim of providing parents with qualifications.

One of the most fascinating observations for the scrutinizers is to compare the work of one pupil in a range of subjects. This will be even more interesting when comparing children's output in the less structured environment of a study support lesson. It may be found that the product of children's endeavours in such an environment is far superior to that produced in the confines of the timetabled day!

One of the difficulties of work scrutiny is not getting bogged down by too much information but, instead, planning out in advance the recording template that will be used so the check is directed and conclusions can be more easily drawn.

Conclusion

There is no doubt that the self-evaluation process for an extended school could easily become an unwieldy or impossible task. Therefore, just as schools will plan their evaluation of the curriculum to take place over a two-year period and move round different subject areas, it is vital to plan your evaluation framework of the extended school. You may choose to use different evaluation tools for different elements of the core offer, depending on their perceived suitability.

Finally, if you are feeling overwhelmed at the thought of evaluating your extended school, it is useful to remember the old phrase that a journey of a 1,000 miles begins with a single step and therefore just make it your aim to start your extended school evaluation, even if it is only one focus group.

Key questions

1. What evidence do you already possess about your extended school?

2. Why do you wish to evaluate your extended school?

3 What extended school activities do you run?

4 Which are the most appropriate tools to evaluate them with?

5 Which staff will be involved in the self-evaluation process?

CASE STUDY 10.2: MONITORING AND EVALUATING A SPECIALIST SCHOOL

When schools complete their first application for specialist school status there is a section of the form, section G, where the school has to explain how the school and community plans would be both monitored and evaluated. For many school leaders this is one of the few occasions were they have to explicitly detail how monitoring and evaluation systems are embedded within the school.

The application for specialist school status is split into two sections: the school section and the community section. The school will have targets appertaining to attainment, curricular provision/take up and enrichment. The community section of the bid is often considered to be in three sections: work with partner primary schools, work with partner secondary schools and work with wider community groups. Due to these discrete sections of the bid, different self-evaluation tools will be used at different times.

Many schools have formed a specialist subject steering group or a specialist college management group which oversees the monitoring and evaluation of the specialist school. This group includes Senior Leaders, Middle Leaders, community partners and, in some cases, governors. This group may not conduct any self-evaluation itself but will co-ordinate the self-evaluation or receive evidence from self-evaluation from others which relates to the specialist status.

The school plan

The school section often gives schools an opportunity to describe their departmental or faculty review process but with the concentration on the curriculum areas which are seen as specialist subjects by the bid.

Data

Due to targets of attainment in the specialist subjects and across the curriculum being set, schools analyse the data at set points during the year to determine whether the school is in-line to meet those targets. Some schools look at prior attainment, target grades, uptake/retention of students, teacher assessments and test results in the light of ethnicity, gender and free school meals on a termly basis to monitor progress towards curriculum area targets.

Observations

Lesson observations are also generally conducted by a wide variety of staff including Senior Leaders and subject leaders and also through peer observation. The results of such observations are collated so that effective strategies and practices can be summarized and then shared with wider staff, either at Senior Leadership meetings, Middle Leadership meetings or staff and department meetings.

Pupil views

Many schools gather the views of pupils on work in the specialist areas and to give this more status and ensure it is regularly repeated, it is conducted by the school council. This also means there is a consistency and progress can be measured by a similar group of pupils being consulted.

When schools implement specific activities for the specialist school, great store is put on asking the pupils for their opinions by ensuring there are evaluation criteria for student events with questionnaires so that effectiveness of the event can be measured.

Feedback

Many specialist schools would expect the director of specialism to complete a report of the progress towards the school targets. Such reports are often written twice a year and draw together data analysis, observations, pupil focus groups and questionnaires to give a coherent sense of the work upon the school plan.

Community plan

Schools often find that, not only is the community plan the hardest to write, it is also the most challenging to monitor and evaluate. The two areas in which schools try to gather data is on the uptake of activities and the effectiveness of the activities. Many community activities will be part of a broad approach to raise skills in particular areas so it is always easy to measure the direct impact on attainment except for discrete community courses.

Data

In terms of data often the key figures are those relating to participation. How many primary school pupils have taken part in a master class? How many partner secondary school pupils have accessed resources on a joint virtual learning environment? How many parents have attended a parent's study support group? There may be attainment data from community classes such as if a maths and computing college is delivering numeracy community classes or if a language college offers evening classes in modern foreign languages.

Observations

Partnership activities that can be observed though the observation materials may be less about the quality of the lesson according to inspection grading and more about the skills related to the specialism which the pupils and students are gaining. If one of the targets within the community plan is working with teachers in partner schools to develop the quality of teaching and learning with appropriate outreach work, it may be appropriate to grade such lessons to determine whether a proportion of partner school lessons are of a required standard. It is often found that community classes are not necessarily observed, however, if the adult learners are being asked to contribute financially to the tuition costs, it is important that quality of teaching and learning are assessed without relying purely on attainment data, especially as it will be rare for such data to consider the starting point of the learner.

Questionnaires

Often a key tool in evaluating community provision is the use of quality assurance questionnaires to ascertain what learners thought about the effectiveness of the activity. Very simple tick sheets could be used with primary school learners and more complex questionnaires with older students or adult learners. Online questionnaires can also be used to determine learners' opinions on certain elements of provision.

Conclusion

Specialist school provision can be very wide and, as a result, its evaluation is not always a simple process. Schools that complete the self-evaluation in the more efficient manner are often focused on the targets they have set themselves and on ensuring the evaluation fits tightly against these. They also make sure that evaluation is an ongoing practice and any activities that are completed by learners are immediately evaluated. Those schools with the best practice will use a common evaluation pro forma to aid making comparisons between different activities.

Key questions

1. What are your key targets?
2. Which of those do you already evaluate through other school systems?
3. What are the most appropriate tools to evaluate other targets?
4. Can you create a common pro forma to evaluate wider activities?
5. Who receives and analyses the evidence?

Evaluating specific aspects of a school

CASE STUDY 10.3: EVALUATING A BEHAVIOUR MANAGEMENT SYSTEM: ARE THEY REALLY GETTING WORSE?

The first few weeks of term are often some of the sunniest of the school year and that brightness is generally matched by a sense of optimism in most schools. The pupils are settling into their new routines and have not yet found their feet. Teaching staff are usually full of energy and their lessons are delivered with matching enthusiasm. New staff are likely to be in a honeymoon period with any difficult pupils who will be trying to understand where the limits are.

How long does it take before that optimism dissipates and you begin to hear comments such as, ' X year is the worst ever' or

'This year's Year 7 is far more challenging than last year' or, probably the most dispiriting, 'The behaviour of the children is getting worse each year'?

Many schools have implemented a variety of systems which teaching staff can use to manage the behaviour of the pupils. Many of these are based on theories of assertive classroom management. This is often designed as a set of staged responses to student ill-discipline in the classroom. The theory is that the majority of pupils told calmly but assertively when their behaviour is unacceptable will conform to the norm. When pupils do not change their behaviour, a set of staged sanctions is implemented, sometimes consisting of various detentions, informing parents and often with the endpoint being removal of the pupil from the classroom.

A central premise of this type of behaviour management system is that, if staff react consistently to pupil misbehaviour, the quality of behaviour will improve as pupils know what is expected of them. Those teachers who lack confidence will be strengthened by a whole school system. It is accepted that such techniques will not work with all pupils, especially those who are on the special needs register for an educational behavioural difficulty.

If it is does appear that teaching is becoming more challenging, two questions can be asked: has pupil behaviour deteriorated? Or is the behaviour management system not being fully effective? Then ask if the system is not working as well as previously, how can it be improved? Rather than waiting for the depths of winter to begin asking these questions when many teachers and leaders are getting snowed under with a multitude of tasks, perhaps the calm start to the term can be used as an opportunity for considering how the quality of behaviour and its management can be evaluated.

Methods of evaluation

The real danger of evaluating behaviour is to concentrate on anecdotes. It is only natural that we will think of the worst pupils we have taught, the most challenging classes or extreme behaviours or incidents from certain pupils. However this does not answer our key questions. Therefore, one of the most challenging tasks in this evaluation is to try to put the anecdotes to one side and try to deal with evidence. The best type of evidence has undergone some triangulation; this means similar conclusions have been found from a number of sources.

Statistics

A starting point for such an evaluation is to consider what statistical evidence is held in the school. The obvious place to begin would be with the numbers of temporary and permanent exclusions. Be careful, though, not to concentrate on figures of extreme behaviour as this is not necessarily a true reflection of a school and, in some cases, it could signify that poor behaviour is dealt with. Moving down the hierarchy of response could be to consider the number of pupils who have been removed from lessons and how often certain pupils have been removed. Are there patterns to be found in the figures, such as peaks for particular year groups, in certain subject areas or with individual teachers? However, these last two figures do not mean that certain subjects or practitioners are less effective than others; it could just be they are sticking more rigidly to the system. Probably what is most interesting is if you have evidence about behaviour in the classroom. Are there particular behaviours being listed? Do pupils begin to behave at a certain point in the hierarchy of response? Are teachers jumping up the ladder of response and not appearing to work through the system? The answers to those questions will enable you to consider the systems that are in place.

What do the pupils think?

We can forget the most important group of people in the process and that is the pupils. They will often tell you where they believe the weak points are in the system and will be able to explain to you when they choose to behave and when they do not. It is generally true that most young people do not want poor behaviour in the classrooms as they do want to learn.

If the statistical analysis highlights a certain year group being poorly behaved or the opposite, being seen as a very positive year group, why not use a questionnaire to find out their views on the behavioural management system? Questions could include:

- What do pupils think of certain sanctions?
- Are there certain points when they will begin to behave?
- How do different teachers use the sanctions?

A questionnaire no longer has to be a sheet of paper which pupils complete in a classroom. Many Virtual Learning Environments have the facility to set up questionnaires on them which pupils can be directed towards when they log onto the system. Such questionnaires are likely to be less influenced by other pupils. A school could even incorporate some kind of reward system so that pupils are encouraged to complete the questionnaire. It is likely that the software will instantly collate statistics too, removing an otherwise laborious chore.

Once you have the results of the questionnaire you may be intrigued by some of the children's responses and wish to probe their beliefs further. A focus group could be an excellent way of gathering this detailed information. It is important to carefully consider which pupils you would use in such a focus group as you will need to gather a cross-section of opinion. If you work with six pupils, one sampling method could be to consider the number of times pupils have received sanctions and select two children who have rarely received sanctions, two children at the other end of the spectrum and two from the middle. It is also important that you carefully plan the questions that you will ask and how you will record their responses.

Working with staff

Staff will have views on the effectiveness of the school's behaviour management system. Remember, though, that it is necessary to move beyond individual anecdotes if you wish to improve the system. The evidence that you have collected and triangulated will be a good way of trying to reduce these types of comments. This evidence could be shared with Middle Leaders, both curriculum and pastoral, and then they could be asked what it reveals about behaviour at the school and how better conditions for learning can be created. There could be three different conclusions: the system needs improving, staff need further training or work needs to be done with pupils to change their behaviours, such as improving their listening skills.

Conclusion

Most importantly, this type of project will move the conversation in the staffroom away from the purely negative idea that behaviour is getting worse and, instead, will focus on how staff can be empowered in a school to deliver the very best teaching and learning. After all, that is what we are all trying to achieve.

Key questions

1. Do you have particular concerns about aspects of your behaviour management system?
2. What evidence do you already possess on behaviour?
3. Which stakeholders' views upon the behaviour management system are you researching? Teachers, pupils, parents, etc?
4. Do you intend to work with a specific sample of stakeholders?
5. Which tools are the most appropriate to gather their views?
6. How will you present your research conclusions?

Evaluation for external awards

The application process for many external awards is often an exercise in self-evaluation. Most external awards have a set of criteria that a school has to show that it has met. For many external awards the key tasks are in selecting the appropriate evidence or in using self-evaluation tools to gain additional information which may be needed to show that certain criteria are met.

> ### CASE STUDY 10.4: THE NACE CHALLENGE AWARD
>
> This is an award which recognizes schools that make excellent provision for more able students. The application process is by no means an easy task and nor is accreditation a foregone conclusion, but the benefits are far reaching. This case study is written in a slightly different style in that it considers the application diary which one school's gifted and talented co-ordinator kept.
>
> *September – deciding to apply*
> The decision to apply for the award was not taken lightly. We decided that not only would an application demonstrate to pupils, parents, governors and the wider community the staff's commitment to stretching the most able, it would also encourage us to audit and review our good practice and action plan to make it excellent.

Being a school on the border of three counties, with their varying school selection procedures and admissions policies, we have always valued highly our truly comprehensive status and been keen to compete with grammar schools and independent schools which are found in the immediate locality.

We wanted parents and prospective parents to know that their children would be able to achieve just as highly with us and we wanted pupils to know that their chances of success were as good as, if not better than, pupils' at neighbouring schools.

A commitment to audit our provision was made by the Senior Team and shared with staff, a subscription to the NACE was taken out (£88 for an average-sized secondary) and the 'Challenge Award Framework' purchased.

We now had access to a range of support materials which gave excellent and thorough advice on good practice, an audit framework, clear guidance on how to make an application and advice on action planning.

October/November – auditing existing provision

Over the next few months we worked hard with staff. There are ten elements against which able, gifted and talented (AGT) provision is judged and all have to be secured.

First comes the compilation of a portfolio of printed evidence and, once this is achieved and passed by NACE assessors, an in-school assessment day follows.

It became clear during this time that while we did some things very well indeed (our extra-curricular programmes, our pathways to learning curriculum design, our work with parents and governors, and staff CPD, for example), we would need to work hard to gather the evidence for other elements.

We used the NACE Framework as an audit tool to evaluate our practice against the criteria, knowing that if we met about 90 per cent of the criteria and had action planned for the rest, then we had a strong case for an application.

December/January 2007 – a whole staff application

It was always important to us to ensure that the Challenge Award and the commitment to support AGT pupils was a whole school undertaking, and we wanted the assessors to see this clearly in our portfolio of evidence. Putting an application together was quite an administrative task; a good few days putting school policy documents into the relevant files.

The first stage was the audit and several meetings with the Deputy Principal were spent logging our ideas for best evidence. Drawing from all aspects of policy and practice, we slowly began to compile a list of evidence to file and gained a sense of what aspects of provision we needed to develop in the school.

We drew up our action plan and by this point had a clear sense of our strengths and of the huge paper mountain we would need to gather. We set ourselves a timeline for completion and this I would strongly recommend to any other colleagues working on a Challenge Award application as the paper chase can seem daunting at times.

Alongside this process, time was given to whole staff briefing and CPD, sharing the progress and benefits of the application with staff and making sure that their input into the process was acknowledged and appreciated. AGT increasingly became a topic for staff discussion, informally as well as in our improvement group meetings.

February to April – the paper trail
Now the paper trail began in earnest, and while the deputy and I constantly gathered evidence to file, other people – including pupils – delivered photos, typed up their views, and gave written accounts of their involvement in school initiatives. Everyone, from the school press officer to parents, heads of departments and governors, contributed to the evidence collection.

Only one official lever arch file can be submitted for the portfolio so, while the evidence had to be comprehensive, it also had to be prioritized. By the end of the month we had lodged our application.

May – disappointment
The NACE recommends 10 –12 weeks between applying and assessment day and asks that the portfolio of printed evidence is submitted four weeks before the assessors visit the school. Our application became ready for submission and on 20 May we proudly handed over a jam-packed file.

The NACE offers a pre-assessment service and for a fee will visit your school to work through the portfolio before it is submitted. So confident were we of the provision at our school, we felt this stage was unnecessary although, on reflection, it was a service we maybe should have taken advantage of. Our disappointment when the portfolio failed to impress the assessors enough to move on to the next stage of the assessment process was significant.

June/July 2007 – getting the portfolio right
One thing we were sure of, and the portfolio assessor assured us about, was that ours was clearly a school that made excellent provision – we just needed to find the right evidence to prove it.

Admittedly, we wondered whether the expectation that so much evidence should be provided on paper was a little old-fashioned. Writing documents for the sake of a place in the file seemed counter-productive, but many of those documents have now proved useful in other areas of school life, providing information in our staff induction packs, for example.

A pre-assessment visit, despite incurring additional cost, gave us invaluable advice from the NACE assessor who later conducted our final assessment. A half-day's meeting and a guided tour of the strengths and weaknesses of our initial portfolio submission proved the ideal leg-up for our new and improved submission, which showed our school in an even better light.

September – re-submission
Not passing the portfolio submission element of the assessment first time meant that our ambition to achieve the award before the start of this academic year was thwarted. We had hoped to promote the school's success in this area with prospective Year 7 parents at our new pupil open evening in early October. Instead we submitted the revised portfolio by the end of the first month of the new academic year and, a week later, were relieved and pleased to hear that the final assessment day was now imminent. 9 October was agreed and the expectations and format of the assessment day made clear in a further telephone conversation with the lead assessor.

October 2007 – assessment day
Interviews with parents, governors, pupils and staff, as well as both planned and random lesson observations and scrutiny of pupils' work, combine to make a busy assessment day.

It started with the arrival of two assessors and a representative from the Local Authority at 8 am and it was made clear to us that the assessment could be aborted at several points during the day if the school's claims of excellence were not supported or borne out during interviews with stakeholders and in lesson observations.

It was a nerve-wracking day indeed, which I spent knowing that I personally could do no more to secure the school's success and, just as in an OFSTED inspection, it was time for the school and its pupils to speak for themselves!

Our stakeholders did us proud and it was incredibly encouraging to know that our parents were so positive about the impact which the school made on their able children's lives.

Staff were nervous but fully appraised and were commended at the end of the day for their massive commitment to pupils. Most endearing of all, of course, were the pupils, who were touchingly loyal and were clearly proud to show off their excellent work and speak at length about their lives as AGT children. The day was not without incident; the assessors spoke with good humour about the challenge provided in a Year 10 mixed-ability RE lesson on the subject of sex before marriage and the Christian faith.

Success!

The announcement at 4 pm, in front of the school's Senior Team and any other interested staff (and there were plenty of them), that our application had been successful was both a relief and a huge vindication of the staff's commitment. Not just commitment to the process of the application, but to all our pupils and the challenge the school provides to help them achieve their very best.

We are now able to do what we set out to do: demonstrate to all the staff's commitment to stretching the most able. The process was undeniably hard work, frustrating at times but, for all that, the award seems even more worthwhile.

Not a hoop-jumping exercise for a logo on our headed notepaper, but a well earned, nationally respected recognition that our able pupils are challenged and supported to be successful, ambitious and high achieving.

Key questions

The following key questions could relate to any external award.

1. What is the motivation in applying for the award?
2. What are the criteria for achieving the award?
3. What evidence is currently held which meets those criteria?
4. Which criteria do you not have evidence for?
5. Which are the most appropriate tools to gather this evidence?

APPENDICES

APPENDIX **2.1**	Using OFSTED Grades for Lesson Observations	150
APPENDIX **2.2**	Lesson Observation Pro Forma	152
APPENDIX **2.3**	Blink Review Lesson Observation Pro Forma	153
APPENDIX **3.1**	Work Scrutiny Pro Forma	155
APPENDIX **6.1**	Pupils Conducting Lesson Observation Pro Forma	156
APPENDIX **8.1**	Maintenance Check Schedule	158
APPENDIX **8.2**	Feedback for Head of Department Pro Forma	159
APPENDIX **8.3**	Pupil Focus Group Questions	161

150 APPENDIX 2.1

	Teaching	
Outstanding (1)	Teaching is stimulating, enthusiastic and constantly challenging. Expert knowledge is shown of the subject, how to teach it and how students learn. Methods are well selected and the pace is good. Activities and demands are matched to student needs and abilities. Both partners in a teaching pair reinforce and support learning. Difficult ideas are taught in an inspiring way and highly effective way.	
Good (2)	The teacher's subject knowledge lends confidence to the teaching style which engages learners and encourages them to work independently. Teaching methods are imaginative and lead to a high level of interest from most students. Work is closely tailored to the full range of learners' needs. There is a wide range of activities. Students are expected to work hard but the level of challenge is realistic, stretching but not inhibiting them. Expectations are high and homework is challenging. Resources including Teaching Assistants are well deployed to support learning. For older students extended projects develops the work in lessons.	
Satisfactory (3)	Teaching is accurate reflecting the teacher's secure knowledge of the curriculum. Teaching is planned to be interesting and varied. Tasks have appropriate challenge to keep students working independently and cooperatively. Provision is made for less well motivated students. Relationships are constructive. Homework extends classwork well. Students can make choices and apply their learning.	
Inadequate (4)	Teaching is dull and does not engage or encourage students. Students do not enjoy their work. Differentiation is insufficient and the level of challenge is not correctly pitched. There is a lack of independent learning or students are passive. Expectations may be low. More effort is given to managing behaviour than learning. Bad behaviour is not adequately managed. The teacher may have an incomplete grasp of the curriculum. Other adults are not appropriately deployed.	

Achievements and standards	Assessment	Attitudes and behaviour
Students are engrossed in their work and make considerably better progress than may be expected. They consider difficult ideas and are willing to tackle challenging topics. Achievement is very high.	Work is assessed thoroughly. Feedback clearly indicates how to improve. Q&A and one-to-one in class support checking and developing understanding. Students are helped to judge their own work and set their own targets. Assessment enables students to play a very strong part in making and recognizing improvements in their work.	Students are happy. They are keen to work and take responsibility for their learning. They are helpful, considerate and consistently behave well. They help each other. There are excellent relationships in the classroom.
Most students make good progress compared to their starting points, meeting challenging targets and achieving high standards. Most groups of learners, including those with learning difficulties and disabilities make at least good progress and some may make very good progress. Learners are gaining knowledge, skills and understanding at a good rate.	Marking is diagnostic, helps students to improve their work and gives teachers a clear grasp of students' knowledge and skills. Oral questions are well targeted to check understanding. Students regularly assess their own work. Assessment findings are used to set challenging student targets.	Most students are interested or absorbed in their work and are eager to achieve well. They are happy to work independently. Behaviour is good and relationships are harmonious.
Most students' learning and achievement are at least satisfactory. Students understand what they are expected to do.	Work is marked regularly and students are aware of the overall quality of what they have done. Teachers know what students have achieved recently. Teachers communicate progress and targets clearly to students.	Most pupils like the subject. They co-operate with the teacher and each other. Behaviour is good and nearly all students are considerate of others. A few students do not remain on-task.
A significant proportion or certain groups make limited progress and underachieve. The pace of learning is insufficient for satisfactory gains in knowledge, skills and understanding. Overall, standards are not high enough.	Assessment is insufficiently used to plan lessons. Marking rarely helps students improve. Recording is unsystematic and not related to progress. Target-setting is based on hunches. Assessment is not frequent, accurate or detailed enough to monitor students' progress so teachers lack understanding of students' needs. Students do not know how to improve.	Most students work willingly on the tasks set but a small minority has a detrimental effect on others. Some have a casual attitude and rely on the teacher for too much input. A significant number of pupils are bored and may behave inappropriately.

Lesson observation pro forma

Copies to: Line Manager, Curriculum Leader, Observee

Name of Observee: _____

Date of Obs: _____

Observer: _____

Class/Set: _____

Subject: _____

Performance Management Target/Focus

(Above to be completed by Observee)

The observer can consult the Middle Leaders' Handbook *for criteria to be considered*

Time	Factors promoting effective learning	Have you considered?
	e.g Planning, Pace, Challenge, Classroom Management, Differentiation, AFL	

Date of Lesson: _____
Date of Feedback: _____

Summary

Was there a particular focus for this observation?

Bearing this in mind, what do you think went well/was effective?

What could have been done differently/better?

In your discussions following this observation, has the teacher identified any specific INSET needs?

Are there particular areas that the teacher could focus on in future:

- with your support?

- independently or with the support of colleagues?

Agreed outcomes from observation:

Signed: _____ (Observer)

Signed: _____ (Observee)

Blink review: lesson observation pro forma

Year: 7 8 9 10 11   Session: 1 2 3

Number of students in class: ____

Male: ☐   Female: ☐

Are all students in correct uniform   Yes   No (Number not in uniform ___)
Do students have planners out on desk?   All   Some   None
Are any students chewing?   Yes   No
Is there a clear rationale for where students are seated?   Yes   No   Not able to ascertain
The classroom environment enhances and is conducive to learning   Strongly agree   Agree   Disagree   Strongly disagree
There are consistent expectations in line with school policies   Strongly agree   Agree   Disagree   Strongly disagree
Based on a 'blink' OFSTED judgement how would you grade the lesson?   Outstanding   Good   Satisfactory   Inadequate
Any brief comments to contextualize the above

Book tracking

		name				
Pupil	presentation – date and title					
	general layout					
	handwriting					
	amount of work					
	corrections					
Teacher	marked to date					
	summative assessment					
	formative assessment					
	targets					
	levels					
	rewards					
Dept	consistency of marking					
	consistency of assessment					
	consistency of presentation					
Comments						

Student observation pro forma

STUDENT VOICE:
Lesson Observation

> Central Foundation Girls' School –
> Educating Tomorrow's Women

Teacher's name: _____   Department: _____ Date: _____

Observer's name: _____   Lesson: _____ Year: _____ Set: _____

ROLE MODELLING e.g. speaks to students with respect, avoids confrontation, body language, punctuality and organization, inspires confidence, high expectations of all, humour, voice (tone, volume, pace)
LESSON PLANNING e.g. logical structure, starter, pace, imaginative activities
DIFFERENTIATION e.g. how suitable is the lesson for G&T, dyslexic, SEN, EAL students? How inclusive is the teacher?
ASSESSMENT e.g. opportunities for reflection and self-evaluation, peer evaluation. Use of higher order questioning. Monitoring progress and understanding during lesson. Quality of marking.
CLASSROOM MANAGEMENT e.g. layout of furniture supports activities, tidiness, students' access to resources, grouping/seating arrangements
BEHAVIOUR MANAGEMENT e.g. relationships, keeping students on task, school rules, handling difficult students, communication, dealing with lates
RESOURCES e.g. use of ICT, whiteboard, OHP, handouts appropriate to learning objectives. Quality of resources: layout, content. Are resources matched to students' abilities?

SUMMARY OF LESSON

KEY POINTS FOR FEEDBACK

SUGGESTIONS

COMMENTS BY TEACHER (OPTIONAL)

Signed: _____ (Observer)

Signed: _____ (Teacher)

Appendix 8.1

Department Maintenance Check Schedule

Department: _____ Dates of Maintenance Check: _____

Review Leader: _____ Date of Analysis meeting: _____ Date of Feedback Meeting: _____

SLT Staff	Department Staff			Marking Sample	Pupil Focus Group	Feedback Meeting
HT						
DH						
DH						
AH						
AH						
SENCO						

HT – Headteacher; DH – Deputy Head; AH – Assistant Head

Feedback for Head of Department Pro forma

Department Maintenance Check

Feedback Sheet 1

Department: _____

Main Strengths:

1)

2)

3)

4)

Issues Arising:

1)

2)

3)

4)

Department Maintenance Check

Feedback Sheet 2

Department: _____

Action Points
1)
2)
3)
Training/Resource Implications

Signed: _____ (SLT)

Signed: _____ (Head of Department)

Date: _____

Pupil Focus Group Questions
Department Maintenance Check Pupil Focus Group

Department: _____

Date: _____

What do you like about this subject?
What type of lessons do you like best?
Do your teachers make you work hard?
Are you making a lot of progress? How do you know?
At what level are you working at present? What is your target level?
Do you know what you have to do to get up to the next level?
Do you have a lot of homework?
Does the homework help you understand the subject?
If you have a problem with the work in this subject do you always feel you can ask for help?
Do you feel safe in your lessons?
Do you feel able to have a go at answering questions even if you may be wrong?
Do you use computers in this subject? What for?
If you could change something about this subject what would it be?

Useful websites & Further reading

Chapter 1
www.ofsted.gov.uk
www.estyn.gov.uk
www.hmie.gov.uk
www.isi.net

Chapter 2
Watson-Davies, R. (2009), *Lesson Observation*. Hampshire: Teachers' Pocketbooks.
Wragg, T. (1999), *An Introduction to Classroom Observation*. London: Routledge.
http://nationalstrategies.standards.dcsf.gov.uk/node/95651

Chapter 3
http://nationalstrategies.standards.dcsf.gov.uk/node/192586
http://nationalstrategies.standards.dcsf.gov.uk/node/97201?uc=force_uj
http://www.effectivemarking.moonfruit.com/

Chapter 4
http://nationalstrategies.standards.dcsf.gov.uk/inclusion/behaviourattendanceandseal/seal/developmentandfocusgroups

Chapter 5
Bernhardt, V. L. and Geise, B., (2009), *From Questions to Actions: Using Questionnaire Data for Continuous School Improvement*. New York: Eye on Education.

Chapter 6
http://www.schoolcouncils.org/freebies/students-as-researchers-observing-lessons-pack/

Chapter 7
Kelly, A. and Downey, C. (2010), *Using Effectiveness Data for School Improvement: A Guide for Managers and Teachers*. London: Routledge.
http://nationalstrategies.standards.dcsf.gov.uk/node/96059

Chapter 8
http://nationalstrategies.standards.dcsf.gov.uk/node/162730

Chapter 9
Kelly, S. (2006), *The CPD Co-ordinator's Toolkit: Training and Staff Development in Schools*. London: Paul Chapman Publishing.
http://nationalstrategies.standards.dcsf.gov.uk/node/175329

Chapter 10
http://www.teachernet.gov.uk/_doc/13099/extendedtoolkit.pdf
www.ssatrust.org.uk
www.nace.co.uk

Index

ALLIS 57, 90
Assessment for learning (AfL) 31, 34, 53, 65, 96, 127
Audit 3, 5, 93, 123, 129, 142, 143, 144
Average Point Score (APS) 4, 5

behaviour management 49, 138, 139–42

capitation 19, 59, 117
Case studies
   A teacher researching their own assessment 64–5
   Adapting the department maintenance check 112–13
   An observation focusing on kinaesthetic learning 26–7
   Analysing G&T classroom practice 66–8
   Annual cycles of lesson observations 15–16
   Assessing the quality of homework 36–7
   'Blink' whole school review 24–5
   Considering the type of teaching 50
   Departmental capitation 59
   Department maintenance check 105–7
   Department mini-SEFs 93
   Evaluating a behaviour management system: are they really getting worse? 138–41
   Evaluating a department's practice 52–3

Case studies (*cont.*)
   Evaluating an extended school 130–4
   Evaluating CPD impact through questionnaires 125–6
   Head of faculty studying performance over time 87–8
   Informal pupil observation feedback 72–3
   Make learning better 76
   Monitoring and evaluating a specialist school 135–8
   School Business Manager assisting with observations 18–19
   Students as learning partners 80–2
   Studying child safety during the school day 54
   Studying G&T pupils' views on extra-curricular provision 44–5
   Subject self-evaluation and subject review procedures 114–18
   Teacher performance 91–2
   Teachers and students co-planning 78–80
   The NACE challenge award 142–6
   The registrar running focus groups 46–7
   Tracking pupil progress at key stage 3 96–7
   Work scrutiny with a focus on continuous writing 35–6
child protection 60
child safety
coaching 6, 20, 28, 29

166 INDEX

coding 38, 54, 61
Cognitive Ability Test (CAT) 4, 5, 90
competency 5, 16, 22, 39
Contextual Valued Added (CVA) 4, 5, 8, 85, 90, 92, 94, 108, 109
Continual Professional Development (CPD) 3, 6, 8, 18, 29, 72, 101–3, 105, 119–128, 129, 133, 143, 144
    At what points can CPD be evaluated? 122, 123
    The link between self-evaluation and CPD 123, 124
    What tools can be used to evaluate CPD? 124–7
    What is Continual Professional Development? 121–2
continuous writing 35, 37

Data, analysing 84–98
    Performance data 89, 90
    How often should the analysis take place 94–7
    Non-academic data 91
    What analysis will be conducted? 92–4
    What is the aim of the data analysis? 86–8
    Who does the data refer to? 88–92

extra-curricular 44–6, 112, 131, 143
Estyn 2
Extended Schools 8, 130–5

Fischer Family Trust (FFT) 4, 5, 8, 90, 96, 114
Focus groups 6, 7, 30, 31, 41, 42–56, 70, 71, 105–7, 112–16, 124, 127, 131, 132, 134, 136, 141
    Analysing comments 53, 54
    Number of pupils 47–9
    Organizing a successful focus group 43–5
    Planning the questions 49–51
    Recording comments 51–3
    Sharing information 54, 55
    Who will be in a focus group 45–7

Gifted & Talented (G&T) 44, 45, 46, 48, 52, 55, 66, 67, 68, 116, 129, 142, 143
Governors 4, 5, 18, 117, 135, 142, 143, 144, 145

Her Majestiy's Inspectorate of Education (HMIE) 2
homework 34–7, 53, 55, 127

INSET 28, 41

Kinaesthetic learning 26

learning walk 5, 24, 26, 27, 112, 133
lesson observation
    Cycle of observations 15, 16, 17
    Duration of observation 22–6
    How will the observations be recorded? 20–2
    Moderation of observation 27
    Observation foci 26, 27
    Using observations to develop teaching and learning 27–9
    What judgements will arise from lesson observations? 20
    Which staff should conduct observations? 17, 18, 19, 20
Likert Scale 60, 64
Literacy Strategy 35, 45

Independent Schools Inspectorate (ISI) 2

MIDYis 90

NACE Challenge Award 5, 9, 130, 142–5
National Strategies 3, 22, 129
NFER 57, 84, 90

OFSTED 1, 2, 5, 6, 18, 21, 25, 26, 27, 39, 40, 42, 44, 47, 86, 97, 102, 103, 107, 112, 114, 130, 133, 146
grades 21

Peer observation 28, 29, 121, 136
Performance Management 3, 16, 17, 23, 24, 26, 85, 93, 105, 107, 114, 125–7
Prep Schools 34
PIPs 90
pupils conducting lesson observations 7, 70–83
    Developing a protocol 73, 74
    Giving feedback 82
    Observers or participants 80–2
    Recording the observation 78–80

pupils conducting lesson observations (*cont.*)
    Selecting and training pupils as observers 74–7
    What are the purposes of pupils conducting lesson observations? 71–3

Questionnaires 7, 43, 57–69, 70, 71, 86, 124, 125, 127, 129–32, 136, 137, 140, 141
    Analysing the data 63–5
    Completing the questionnaires 62, 63
    Formulating the questions 60, 61
    Presenting the results 66–8
    The aim of the questionnaire 58, 59
    Which pupils will be involved? 61, 62

Raise Online 92–94

Schon, Donald 4
School Business Manager (SBM) 18, 19, 59, 106
School Council 74, 136
School Development Plan 24
School Improvement Partner 1, 22, 24, 85, 87, 97
Self-Evaluation Form (SEF) 1, 2, 26, 101, 102, 103, 105, 117, 130
    Mini-SEFs 93, 94, 107, 108, 114, 116
Self-Evaluation Report 2
Special Educational Needs 3
Specialist Schools 81, 129, 136

Teaching and Learning Responsibility (TLR) 3
Teaching and Learning Review Systems 8, 91–118
    How will the date be analysed? 113
    How will the information be shared? 113–18
    The frequency of reviews 112, 113
    What sections is the school being divided into? 103, 104
    Which self-evaluation tools will be used? 104–7
    Who will be involved? 107–12
    Why is the evidence being gathered? 103
Tracking 8, 85, 95, 96, 97, 114, 116, 131
Triangulation 5, 16, 41, 43, 53, 54, 93, 101, 102, 104, 131, 139

Virtual Learning Environments (VLE) 6, 62, 68, 140

Woodward, Clive 2
Work scrutiny 6, 30–41, 42, 43, 48, 49, 105, 106, 107, 112, 113, 116, 127, 131, 134
    Feedback 38–40
    Focus 33–6
    Organization 32–3
    Writing up 36–8

Year Eleven Information Service (YELLIS) 4, 5, 7, 8, 57, 90, 92, 132